An Introduction to Politics

An Introduction to Politics

Lectures for First-Year Students

Third Edition

Trevor Munroe

Canoe PRESS

BARBADOS • JAMAICA • TRINIDAD and TOBAGO

Canoe Press
1A Aqueduct Flats   Mona
Kingston 7   Jamaica

CATALOGUING IN PUBLICATION DATA

Munroe, Trevor St George.
   An introduction to politics : lectures for first-year
   students / Trevor Munroe. – 3d ed.

   p. cm.

   ISBN: 978-976-8125-79-8

   1. Political science – Study and teaching –
   Caribbean, English-speaking. 2. World
   politics. I. Title.

   JA88.J3M86 2002   320.9

Book design by Roy Barnhill.
Cover design by Robert Harris.

Contents

SECTION IV
The Presidential and Parliamentary Systems of Government

SECTION V
The Transition from Communism and Post-Communism

APPENDIX

Tables and Figures

TABLES

FIGURES

Preface

The third edition of *An Introduction to Politics* comes a little over nine years after the publication of the second edition in June 1993. This second edition, I am informed, has sold more copies than any other publication of the University of the West Indies Press. For this, I am truly grateful and wish to record sincere appreciation to the thousands of students, scholars, and ordinary citizens who over the years have made positive remarks as well as constructive criticisms of that book.

A new edition has become necessary because much has changed in the world of politics over the last decade. Hence this edition explores more fully relatively new issues relating to political culture, political behaviour, democracy, globalization, and Caribbean politics. It sheds light on Caribbean and global phenomena such as increasing disaffection with politics, growing abstention from voting, and rising levels of protest, largely in response to complex challenges posed to small island states by the imbalances in power at the national and international levels.

This third edition draws on material from many sources otherwise difficult for students to access. As was the case with the earlier editions, a main purpose of the book is to provide readers with a cost-effective means of learning the basics of political studies.

This edition has been produced in record time. For this, many thanks are due to Linda Speth, director of the University of the West Indies Press; Shivaun Hearne, managing editor with the University of the West Indies Press; and to Christine Cummings, Charlene Sharpe-Pryce, Donna Hope, and Paul Kenyon, my colleagues in the Department of Government at the University of the West Indies Press, Mona, whose help was, in different ways, invaluable. To Adlyn Smith and Jennifer Jackson-Hill, special thanks for assistance in typing the manuscript. Finally, I acknowledge with appreciation the encouragement of students and staff alike in the course of writing the book.

Kingston
August 2002

Introduction

This book is divided into seven sections and we summarize them here.

Section 1 is "Political Behaviour, Political Culture, and Political Socialization". We will explain the meanings of these terms and their significance to the study of politics.

In section 2 we look at the definition of political science. What does that subject entail? What does the term political science really mean? At the end of that, we are going to see that the meaning of political science and the meaning of politics have changed significantly over the years. We are going to see how it has changed, what it means now, what accounts for that change, and, most significantly, how it is likely to change in the future.

In section 2 you will see that understanding politics and political science is extremely important in paving your way, whatever your chosen career. Whether you become a businessperson, professional, or academic, this course will help you to understand the environment and its context that impacts on you.

Section 3 is perhaps one of the most fundamental elements in our course. Certainly, the most significant part of any course in political science in any university deals with the issue of democracy. These days we hear so much about human rights. What are these human rights? What do they do? What is democracy? We will look at questions such as, Is Jamaica a democracy? What is it that makes the United States a democracy, if indeed it is? What are some of the dimensions of life in these countries that need to be changed if they are to be better governed as democracies and if the rights of the people are to be more recognized and advanced?

We are going to define democracy and the different types of democracy. Representative democracy is one type, the kind of democracy that exists in the United Kingdom, the United States, France, Jamaica, and Barbados. We will also look at participatory democracy, where much rests on the participation – the involvement – of the people themselves directly, not being so dependent on their political representatives. We are going to look at this distinction between representative and participatory democracy. We will see how many countries in the world are democratic; how many are not; how far some countries have changed from being democratic to being undemocratic, and how far in the other direction have countries that were undemocratic become democratic. This is a very significant part of the course. We will also look at the different types of governmental structures in democracies.

Section 4 looks at the differences and similarities between the US presidential and the British parliamentary systems. We will look at the differences in how these two major types of government are organized and how decisions are made.

Section 5 examines the transition from communism and looks at post-communism. In this section we look at the products of this system that emerged in the modern world; that is, the communist system, how it happened, why it happened, and, most importantly from our point of view, what has happened since the collapse of that system. What is happening today in the republics that were communist? Do the people believe they are better off, or do they believe they are better off in some respects and worse off in others? We will look at opinion polls that have been taken in those countries, in which people express their views regarding their position.

Section 6 is about the Caribbean. The central purpose of this section is to acquaint you with Jamaican and Caribbean forms of government, to make you aware of the global reality in which the countries of the Caribbean operate, because, these days, increasingly, what is local is global and what is global is local. In section 6 we also discuss proposals for constitutional reforms in the Caribbean.

In section 7 we look at contemporary Caribbean politics from the standpoint of globalization. We will try to understand the meaning of globalization. We will consider regionalism and what it means and why it is important that the region cooperates more closely. What is the Caribbean Community and what opportunities does it present, and what are the dangers? We will consider a single Caribbean market and economy as part of regionalization – this would be similar to the market between Westmoreland and Kingston and St Andrew, where labour can move from Kingston to Savanna-la-mar or vice versa. We also look at political change. What is necessary? Why is it important to change the politics so the region can move forward and achieve the benefits?

POLITICAL BEHAVIOUR, POLITICAL CULTURE, AND POLITICAL SOCIALIZATION

1

POLITICAL BEHAVIOUR

Political behaviour may be defined as any action regarding authority in general and government in particular. This authority includes church, school, and any others but in particular governmental authority. An obvious example of an act of political behaviour is the act of voting. In casting your vote you are, in a democracy, relating to government by voting for whom you feel should form the government. In this act of political behaviour, you also decide who you do not want to form the government. However, there are other acts of political behaviour that we need to identify, particularly because they are becoming more prevalent in Jamaica, the Caribbean, and around the world. I refer to protests, demonstrations, and roadblocks, which are acts of political behaviour because they relate to some authority. Examples of these authorities are government in general, or some other authority that provides water, fixes the roads, or upholds the law. To sharpen our understanding it is necessary to distinguish political behaviour from two other types of behaviour, economic behaviour and social behaviour.

Economic behaviour may be defined as any action relating to the marketplace: any act of production, consumption, or distribution – the producing, buying, or selling of goods and of services. When you go into the bookshop and purchase the *Introduction to Politics* text, you are engaging in an act of economic behaviour. Any action relating to the market is appropriately called economic behaviour.

Social behaviour is more general. Social behaviour relates to interaction – interrelationships not involving economic transactions or authority of any kind, governmental or otherwise. For example, when you leave this classroom and encounter a gathering of students, what takes place there is social behaviour. Social behaviour is a very important part of life, because it is how we deal with one another. If we have an argument or a difference of opinion, how do we deal with that difference of opinion? Do we curse, exchange violent words or deeds, or do we seek to come to some understanding of each other's views? Social behaviour is very crucial to setting the tone of life around us.

Having made these distinctions, we need to recognize that there are relationships among these categories of behaviour. So, while we understand that they are separate we must also understand that they are connected. There is a connection between political behaviour and economic behaviour. For example, many people may choose not to vote – an act of political behaviour. They may choose not to vote because of their particular economic situation – whether they voted, or their father, grandfather, and great-grandfather before them voted, that political behaviour sometimes has not changed their economic situation. Hence, they have a disinclination to vote. Therefore, the economic condition feeds back into making them not vote. Therefore, we should understand that political behaviour and economic behaviour are connected. The opposite example is of those who benefit from contracts to build a sidewalk or to clear a patch of ground, or help to build a school, engaging in an economic activity and by virtue of benefiting from that economic activity may also engage in political behaviour.

If we are economically distressed and frustrated, unable to find work, unable to purchase food, we are not likely in our social interactions with others to be gentle or understanding. Hence, at times we tend to be aggressive, as a result of frustration with our inability to meet basic needs. We see that social behaviour is often connected to economic circumstances. On one radio talk show it was acknowledged that, while Jamaica's suicide rate is increasing, it is also a fact that the rate is one of the lowest in the world, much lower than that of the United States and Trinidad. This increase is being attributed to economic frustrations and personal loss of various kinds. This example is given in order to dramatize the link between social behaviour, in that case, a very personal form of social behaviour in which someone takes his or her own life, and the economic dimension of the circumstances in which we find ourselves.

POLITICAL PARTICIPATION

A major form of political behaviour is *political participation*. Political participation is defined as the extent to which citizens use their rights, such as the right to protest, the right of free speech, the right to vote, to influence or to get involved in political activity. Political participation can be subdivided into:

1. *Conventional political participation*, which takes place within the norms and traditions of a particular country; therefore, we say it is normal, conventional, and customary. By and large it is the less aggressive of the two. The best example is the act of voting. Other forms of conventional political participation include attending a political meeting, being a member of a political group or a political party.

2. *Unconventional political participation* tends to move outside the norm, move outside the traditional, and be more aggressive, more assertive, and may even break the law. It is also more radical. The best examples are protests and demonstrations that are confrontational rather than peaceful.

Voting (conventional) and roadblocks (unconventional) are forms of political participation because in each case the citizen is using a right to act: in one case the right to vote and in another case the right to assembly and the right to march.

In relation to conventional political participation, we have identified elections and the use of the right to vote. A very interesting development in political behaviour is that in Jamaica and across the Caribbean, voting as a conventional expression of political participation is in decline. The percentage of persons who vote is decreasing as a general trend in Jamaica and across the Caribbean region. In "Caribbean Thought and the Political Process"[1] the data on voting in the Caribbean shows that in the 1990s the average percentage of people turning out to vote in the region was approximately 65 percent (see Table 1.1). This average includes Antigua and Barbuda, St Kitts and Nevis, Grenada, Trinidad and Tobago, Barbados, and Jamaica. The average turn out to vote in the 1980s was approximately 74 percent and in the 1970s it was even higher.

In the 1940s, elections were relatively new, as Jamaica was the first predominantly black country in the entire world where people won adult suffrage, ahead of Asia, Africa, and the rest of the Caribbean. After the 1970s there was a decline in voter participation, and that is not just a Jamaican phenomenon but a regional one. More interestingly, this pattern of conventional political participation exemplified by percentage voter turnout is not Jamaican or regional only. It is also global.

With small variations, you will find a similar pattern in the United States, the United Kingdom, and other industrialized countries. This is particularly interesting, from two points of view. One is that many Jamaicans believe in the simple conclusion that not voting is a reflection of economic underdevelopment. If not voting was simply a matter of economic underdevelopment, then the United States would have the highest voter turnout in the world as it is the most economically developed. But in fact fewer people voted in the last two presidential elections in the United States than for the previous 75 years. Fewer people voted then in that country, measured by percentage, than in the Jamaican elections. Clearly low voter turnout is explained by more than simple economics.

Another explanation is that people are apathetic or neither interested in politics nor in voting anymore and are indifferent. The difficulty with that conclusion is that, while conventional political participation is declining, unconventional political participation as a type of political

Table 1.1   Commonwealth Caribbean: Average Electoral Turnout
1950s–1990s

Country	1950s	1960s	1970s	1980s	1990s
Antigua & Barbuda	64 (2)	48 (2)	86 (2)	67 (3)	63 (2)
Monsterrat	–	47 (2)	77 (3)	73 (2)	67 (1)
St Kitts & Nevis	–	68 (2)	80 (2)	73 (3)	66 (1)
Dominica	74 (3)	79 (2)	79 (2)	77 (2)	65 (2)
Grenada	69 (3)	68 (3)	74 (2)	86 (1)	62 (3)
St Lucia	55 (3)	52 (2)	76 (2)	64 (3)	63 (1)
St Vincent & the Grenadines	67 (3)	81 (3)	67.5 (3)	81 (2)	66.5(2)
Barbados	62 (2)	70 (2)	78 (2)	74 (2)	60 (2)
Jamaica	66 (2)	77.5 (2)	82 (2)	83 (2)	66 (2)
Belize	–	72.5 (2)	80 (2)	74 (2)	72 (1)
Trinidad & Tobago	75 (2)	77 (2)	56 (1)	61 (2)	66 (1)
Averages	66 (20)	68 (24)	76 (23)	74 (24)	65 (17)

Parentheses indicate the number of elections on which the average is based. The
percentages are rounded.

Source: Munroe, "Caribbean Thought and the Political Process", 238.

behaviour is increasing. How do you explain that often the same people
who are indifferent or apathetic to voting may well be involved in massive protests and demonstrations? Unconventional political participation
is increasing in many countries and is also rising in relation to global
organizations and not just national ones. In *Renewing Democracy*,[2] I
tracked protests and demonstrations in Jamaica. In 1989 there were about
20 protests/roadblocks, which increased to 200 by 1997.

Therefore, a major issue in political science and for the citizen who
wants to understand what is happening around him or her is to try to
explain this apparent contradiction. In the following chapter we continue
to search for fuller understanding of this phenomenon. We will examine
the concept of *political culture*. In the same way we see political behaviour
changing, political culture is also changing. The change in political culture is one of the factors in bringing about a change in political behaviour.

NOTES

1. Trevor Munroe, "Caribbean Thought and the Political Process", in
   Contending With Destiny, ed. Ken Hall and Denis Benn (Kingston: Ian
   Randle Publishers, 2000), 238.
2. Trevor Munroe, *Renewing Democracy into the New Millennium: The Jamai-
   can Experience in Perspective* (Kingston: The Press, University of the
   West Indies, 1999).

2

POLITICAL CULTURE

Political culture means the attitudes, feelings, ideas, and values that people have about politics, government, and their own role, and more generally about authority in all its various forms. When we put it that way, we immediately see that every country has a political culture. I suppose too that there is no country without a music culture – people having a different attitude towards a certain type of music and a certain attitude towards music they do not like. Similarly, political culture is a universal phenomenon and it varies from one country to another; thus, the political culture in the United States is different in some ways from the political culture in Jamaica because the attitudes, feelings, and values of those people towards politics and towards their own roles is different from ours. The attitude of US citizens toward politics may be different from that of the British or the French. Therefore, you cannot understand the politics of any country without looking at the political culture of the people.

It is important to clarify this at the very beginning because otherwise we may get confused. We will say things like England has the same form of government as Jamaica – they have the same governmental structure; they have a prime minister, we have a prime minister; they have a parliament, we have a parliament. In that sense the governmental structure is very similar, if not identical. But if we were to move from that to say that because our governmental structures are very similar, even identical, our politics are very similar, we would be making a serious mistake because between the structures and the politics is the *culture* – how people feel. How an English person feels about his or her political party, prime minister, parliament, or elections may be very different from how the Jamaican feels about these, even though they are very much the same type in the two countries.

Similarly, it is very important to understand that political cultures change in the same country over different periods. The political culture in one country is different from that in another country, although there may be common factors. In addition, the political culture in Jamaica in

2002 may be very different in many respects from the political culture in Jamaica in 1982.

The distinction between political culture and political behaviour is important, and we examine this below.

POLITICAL CULTURE AND POLITICAL BEHAVIOUR

Political behaviour refers to action or inaction – what you do or do not do in relation to politics and government. Political culture, in contrast, refers to the dimension of ideas and beliefs, which are in your head and are not easy to see. Political behaviour is easy to track. Political culture, because it refers to a belief system, to attitudes and feelings, is a little more difficult and complex.

Again, we see that, while these two concepts are different, they are also related. We are all aware of the maxim, "by their deeds we shall know them"; perhaps one could say, "by their political behaviour (their deeds), we can know their political culture (their beliefs)". This would be too simple, however, because we may also say that very often we behave in ways that are not consistent with our beliefs. Very often, we do things that we justify as being caused by circumstances rather than our convictions. For example, if I said that Jamaicans are undisciplined, it could mean that Jamaicans do not behave in a disciplined way – referring to the dimension of behaviour. It could also mean that Jamaicans do not value discipline at all. Therefore, if they are put in a framework that requires discipline they will rebel.

Several years ago when there was a minibus system in Jamaica, if we were to conclude on the character of the people from their approach to getting onto the minibuses, you would say they were a bunch of hooligans who did not believe in order and rejected any kind of discipline. Were this true, however, we would have had a rebellion against a more disciplined approach when the minibus system changed. Circumstances make us behave in a particular way, which may not be consistent with our beliefs. While behaviour, and political behaviour in particular, is related to beliefs, they are not the same, because behaviour may arise out of circumstances, whereas belief arises out of conviction. This is important not just in terms of analysis but in terms of policy if the intention is to change behaviour.

Changing behaviour is generally much simpler and less complex than changing values and convictions. For example, if we state that Jamaican political culture is violent, that is a different statement from saying that Jamaican political behaviour is violent. Political behaviour may be violent, especially in certain communities, but people may not necessarily want to conduct their politics by violence. It may be because of the political circumstances of the communities in which they live. If you move these people from inner-city Kingston to Brooklyn or Miami, they may not necessarily have the same orientation toward violence, because that is not their conviction. It is more the circumstances in which they find themselves that lead some of them to resort to violence.

Therefore, public policy has to be different, if you are trying to change political beliefs or any other belief. A massive educational effort is necessary to achieve this aim. Trying to change behaviour is more related to modifying the framework – the circumstances. For example, once we had a one-year system at the University of the West Indies, where there were exams once each year, in May. The beginning of the academic year was in September/October and there were no mid-semester or end-of-semester exams. How did students behave? Because of this framework, little or no work was done by the majority of students until April each year. The framework provided the incentive to work in May. The library was more or less empty up until March or April; the study spots on campus were empty. The change to the semester system meant mid-semester exams in October, end-of-semester exams in December, mid-semester exams in March, and end of semester exams in May. The behaviour of students changed dramatically. Their behaviour changed, not so much because their beliefs and values had been modified but the circumstances or the framework had shifted.

In our examination of political culture, we shall look at four dimensions:

1. Attitudes and values in general
2. Attitudes to political and national institutions
3. Attitudes to political identity
4. Attitudes to leadership

ATTITUDES AND VALUES

These two words, *attitudes* and *values*, mentioned in the definition of political culture, may seem to be more or less the same on first encounter, but they are somewhat different. The difference is that attitudes are relatively temporary. A person's attitude today may be different from his or her attitude tomorrow, because attitudes may change over time. Values are more enduring. For example, attitudes to voting on a particular occasion may be very negative, for any number of reasons. Voters may not see the candidates as worth voting for, but at some time in the future a candidate or group may inspire the confidence of voters and that attitude toward voting could change. The *value* placed on the right to vote is quite a different matter.

The majority of students in this course over 18 years old may consider not voting, because they do not see anyone worth voting for at the present time. Suppose, however, that there was a military take-over and Jamaicans could no longer exercise the right to vote. You would find quite a negative response from a large number of Jamaicans, who would not be prepared to have their right to vote taken away. You can see that your attitude to voting may change, depending on whether there is anything you regard as worth voting for, but the value you place on the right to vote is high and is one that endures, even though you may not exercise it. Attitudes change and values remain and political culture is made up of both.

Political culture is an extremely important dimension of politics that has not been adequately studied.

Political Values

Value means that which is considered worthwhile. Generally speaking, in the world of 2002 and for the last decade or two, in our country and around the world a primary value is placed on democracy. By holding democracy in high regard we are also choosing not to value *dictatorship*. In a dictatorship some external power tells you what to do, when to do it, and how to do it. By and large in the modern world, values have shifted strongly against dictatorship and in favour of democracy. However, within that concept of democracy there are a number of elements that we also value as subsets of democracy.

- Freedom: We value the ability to go where we want, when we want, how we want, without restriction. We value the ability to say what we want, how we want, and when we want. We value freedom of worship and freedom of speech.
- Justice: By justice we mean fair play.
- Better living: Improved living conditions is highly valued.
- Equality: We value equality and not vast inequalities.
- Rule of law: We value law and order because this is supposed to give us a certain amount of personal security. We feel secure because the more law and order there is the more we feel free from being criminally attacked.

In terms of values, democracy in general and these subsets specifically reflect values that we each accept and uphold to one degree or another. The difficulty arises when we try to rank these values. What weight would you attach to freedom as against equality? What weight do you attach to justice as against personal security and law and order? When you begin to assign weights to these values you encounter differences among individuals and, more significantly, differences among social classes, as well as among countries, because each might rank these subsets of democracy differently.

Understanding how these values are ranked becomes important in understanding political culture. For example, each of us values our freedom but we also value our personal security. Suppose you are unable to have both at the same time, to the same extent, how far would you be willing to give up one for the other? Would you be prepared to sacrifice your freedom to go out in Kingston and St Andrew because of curfews preventing us from going out after 6:00 p.m. Monday through Sunday, in order to ensure greater personal security? Would your values allow you to live with less freedom in order to allow the security forces more opportunity to hold the gunmen? It is important to know your political culture, therefore. Imagine that you were a policy maker who thought that the people's first priority was to get rid of crime and that meant imposing a curfew after 6:00 p.m. If you pass a law to that effect and that is not what the people want it would mean you have misunderstood the political culture. Even if this is the political culture in Nigeria, Pakistan, or Barbados, it would not necessarily be the political culture in Jamaica.

If crime and violence continues, and personal freedom has to be sacrificed in order to address the problem, then the need will arise for analysis of the political culture. For example, in Jamaica and elsewhere, new laws are being passed regarding the tapping of telephones. You cannot get at the drug dons and the international narcotics traffickers unless you are able to intercept their communication more effectively. But intercepting communications in the interest of national security and reduction in crime potentially interferes with personal privacy and personal freedom. Again, you may value your personal privacy and freedom above the necessity to deal more effectively with crime, however bad it becomes.

We conclude by saying how different people order their preferences is one distinguishing and defining feature of political culture. I would guess that the primary value in the Caribbean would be freedom, with justice not too far behind. It is not difficult to understand why, as for most of our history we were slaves.

ATTITUDES TO POLITICAL AND NATIONAL INSTITUTIONS

Generally, studies that have been done suggest that the institutions in which the Jamaican people place great confidence and value are the media (radio, television, newspaper), followed closely by the church. The last major survey was done in 1995 by a graduate student in the Department of Government and it showed that the media was a little ahead of the church as the institution Jamaicans regarded as the most important. Third were social organizations, such as sporting associations, youth clubs, and citizens associations and fourth, trade unions representing workers trying to get better working conditions and improved wages. Last of all were political parties.

In Latin America 77 percent of the people expressed confidence in the church and 20 percent confidence in a political party. Similarly in the United Kingdom, the United States, and other industrialized countries, the value placed on political institutions as part of the political culture has been falling significantly over the last 20 to 30 years.[1]

To summarize, studies of the second dimension of political culture – attitudes toward institutions – reveal the general tendency for confidence in political institutions and trust in political parties to be declining in our region, hemisphere, and, generally, across the world.

The terrorist attack against the United States, which destroyed the World Trade Center and part of the Pentagon, was an act of political behaviour. Political behaviour is an action or failure to act in relation to government or authority in general. We saw earlier that political participation was identified as a form of political behaviour, of which there are two types – conventional and unconventional. The argument that terrorism is an unconventional form of political participation is justified by the fact that terrorism can be defined as the use of indiscriminate violence for a political purpose by an individual or group against innocent people or non-combatants. The argument that terrorism is unconventional political participation is based on the point of view that it is seeking to attain a political end and therefore it is similar to a demonstration.

On the other hand, the argument against that point of view is that political participation involves the use of rights – the right of freedom of speech, the right to protest, the right to vote – and therefore since terrorism involves violence it is not a right. No one has the right to use violence against innocent people, and therefore it is not properly classified as political participation.

Based on the events of September 11, 2001 in relation to values and preferences, the American people and government are trying to decide how to balance the value of freedom against the need for security. The World Trade Center attack was one of the purest forms of terrorism, whereas the attack on the Pentagon could be seen as somewhat different because it could have been regarded as directed at a military establishment with combatants and not just innocent people, as the individuals in the World Trade Center were.

ATTITUDES TO POLITICAL IDENTITY

When we consider the element of *identity* in political culture we are looking at three different dimensions:

1. The way in which people define themselves
2. The extent of attachment to a national identity
3. The basis of that attachment

The Primary Points of Reference by Which People Define Themselves

What is the main way in which an individual, the members of a group, or a people see themselves? This becomes an issue because each of us has different aspects to our identity. We have a gender aspect, we each belong to a particular racial or ethnic group, we each are born in some geographic location, we each, generally speaking, uphold some religious belief, and we each live and work in a particular country. Therefore, how you define yourself in terms of one or another of these is of great significance in determining your identity.

For example, if we met in Miami International Airport and I asked, "Who are you?", you may say, "I am John Brown from Jamaica" or "I am a Jamaican." You immediately would turn to Jamaica, Barbados, or Trinidad as your primary point of reference. You may say, "Why do you ask me that? I am a black man." Immediately the point of reference is not a nationality, but a colour, race, or ethnicity. If you asked another person who he is, he may say, "I am a Muslim", because religious affiliation is that person's primary self-definition. Therefore, in analysing the political culture of any people or the political culture of a people at different points in time it is important to determine what is their primary allegiance, what is their primary self-definition. Is it racial, is it religious, is it geographic, or is it political?

In the Caribbean, people define themselves primarily according to their island identity, whether they are Jamaican, St Lucian, or Barbadian, and they do so more than in relation to any other identity, more so than in relation to their racial character or their religious affiliation. Therefore, in terms of identity the Caribbean territories are relatively homogeneous. Part of the issue that modern politics is confronting is whether that homogeneous definition based on geographical island identity is being split up by tribal politics, that is, that people are seeing themselves, at least in some sections of the society, more in terms of their party identities than in terms of their "Jamaicanness" or their "Trinidadianness".

The Extent of Attachment to a Particular National Identity

There are two contending points of view in respect of the Caribbean. The first is that there is a strong attachment to national identity. The evidence in support of this is, first of all, taken from public opinion surveys, which suggest that Caribbean individuals are very attached to their island identity. Second is the extent to which they return if they do emigrate.

No matter how long they live in the United States or Canada they preserve their "Jamaicanness", their "Trinidadianness" or their "Guyanese" character. They preserve it in all kinds of ways – in the food they eat, the music they love, and the visits they make to the Caribbean when they have the opportunity.

In Jamaica, for example, there are about 1 million tourists who come here every year, and over 100,000 of those are Jamaicans who live and work abroad and who, because of their attachment to their Jamaican identity, return whenever they have a vacation opportunity. They also return to retire or, even before retirement age, to work. Jamaicans residing overseas also send money home. These remittances are approximately US$600 million per year. This is about five times earnings from the sugar industry and close to revenues from bauxite/alumina and tourism.

On the other hand, and in opposition to the preceding argument, is the view that the attachment is far from strong; it is rather very superficial and conditional. Evidence supporting this position is the extent of emigration. Statistics show that the Caribbean has the highest percentage in the world of its people living outside of their geographic region. The argument is that this willingness to emigrate constitutes a sign of superficial attachment. In 1999, the US embassy in Kingston granted 11,500 migrant visas to Jamaicans. Remember the Jamaican population is approximately 2.6 million. The country granted the largest number of migrant visas is Mexico, which in 1999 received 56,000 migrant visas. The population of Mexico is approximately 95 million, which means that the population of Mexico is about 35 times that of Jamaica but the number of visas issued is about 5 times the number of those issued in Jamaica. In effect, Jamaicans are getting migrant visas to the United States 7 times more than the Mexicans. In India, with a population of 1,000 million people, 28,000 migrant visas were granted in 1999. The extent of emigration from Jamaica to the United States is close to number one of all the countries in the world in relation to population.

Proponents of this viewpoint also cite the evidence that, all other things being equal in the Caribbean, people will select a foreign consumer item over a local one, even if the local product is of the same or of better quality.

Thus, in relation to national identity, the extent of attachment is a matter of controversy. There is evidence to suggest that attachment to national identity is deep but there is also evidence to suggest that the attachment is weak and conditional.

The Basis of Attachment

In the United States the basis of attachment and pride in country is clear. This has to do with the so-called American Dream: the belief that the United States is a land of opportunity, a land of the free, and the idea that no matter where you were born you can reach to the top.

In the United Kingdom the basis of attachment is different. People identify with the historical achievements of Britain. In our case, studies have shown that the basis that makes us proud of our identity is not politics or economic achievement. The basis of identity is our sporting and cultural achievements (for example, our music). In addition, we take pride in the beauty of our island (environment).

ATTITUDES TO LEADERSHIP

A working definition of *leadership* would be the ability of an individual or group to move others to action, or to agree on a particular course, mainly by non-coercive means. This concept of leadership involves at least two dimensions: followers and leaders. In looking at political culture as this relates to leadership, we identify two qualities that define the leader–follower relationship: deference and egalitarianism.

The Quality of Deference

In a deferential relationship, the follower defers to the leader. Conversely, the leader expects or demands that the follower will go along with whatever he or she says. This relationship may be based on one of a number of different types of leadership. Usually, political scientists recognize three types of leadership that reflect deference between followers and leaders: charismatic, paternalist, and managerialist.

Charismatic Leadership

The charismatic leader is one who regards himself or herself as a saviour. More important, this leader is regarded by those who follow as being a deliverer or saviour or, as some would say, a prophet. The charismatic leader is usually perceived as having a special gift. The nature of this gift will vary according to cultures and situations. In the Old Testament of the Bible, for example, the charismatic leaders were regarded as having gifts in so far as they were the spokespersons of God. Other charismatic leaders are regarded as having special gifts to bring about results. Common to charismatic leaders is that they are set apart and they set themselves apart from the majority of persons who follow them. It may well be that charisma is associated with eloquence, or with a certain physical bearing. Whatever the source, the result is that this is a very special person who requires very special followers because he or she is gifted with special qualities of leadership and of guidance.

Paternalist Leadership

The term paternalist comes from the original Latin, *pater*, which means father. We get the adjective paternalist, which means that this type of leader is a parental or father figure. Because he is a father or parental figure he must be obeyed, listened to, and followed. The paternalist may be quite different from the charismatic leader. The charismatic leader is effervescent and has the gift of speech and all of the other associated characteristics but the paternalist is simply regarded as the father of the nation, or as the father of the particular group, religious or otherwise, and therefore is someone who needs to be given total obedience and total respect.

Managerialist Leadership

As we would say in Jamaican, he is simply the boss. The boss is someone who is set upon a pedestal, and the followers are beneath, and must listen to him or her and follow orders.

In each of these three cases, the leader knows it all and is wiser, better informed, more gifted, more experienced and therefore you need to do, think, and feel as he or she says. In this kind of deferential relationship, disagreement with the leader is unusual, extraordinary, and when it occurs, is not tolerated. Those who disagree with the leader do so at their peril. They are expelled from the organization, disciplined, or suspended. Some form of sanction accompanies disagreement.

This type of leadership predominated in the past in Caribbean political culture. Between the 1940s and 1970s the dominant political culture accepted that leaders were charismatic, paternalist, or managerialist and citizens/followers had little or no right to disagree, followed whatever they said, and supported whatever they did. The classic leader of this type would have been Jamaica's Sir Alexander Bustamante. He both required and attracted such absolute support that you may have heard of the song, "We will follow Bustamante until we die". In Trinidad and Tobago, Dr Eric Williams attracted a similar relationship of deference. The story goes that whenever he appointed a member of his Cabinet, the new member would be required to submit to him as leader an undated letter of resignation, so that if the minister of government stepped out of line, Williams would simply put in the date and the resignation would become effective. Vere Bird in Antigua and Eric Gairy in Grenada are also examples of this type of leader.

Egalitarianism

In an egalitarian relationship the leader and followers regard each other as relatively equal. The leader is respected and valued but he or she is not seen as being up on a pedestal with everyone else down below.

In egalitarian relations the followers also regard themselves as having legitimate positions and opinions, which the leader needs to hear and take into account. This type of leader–follower relationship is participatory.

By this, we mean that the leader expects the followers to participate actively in decision making. The leader expects the followers to present their views. The leader not only tolerates disagreement but values different points of views. In this kind of relationship the leader is not a general, a prophet or a saviour, he or she is more the captain of a team who understands that the participation of every member of the team is important. This leader knows that as "team captain", he or she needs and must encourage the different skills and talents of the members of the team.

From the 1980s onwards, in my opinion, the citizens and particularly the younger people in Jamaica and the Caribbean are less responsive to the type of leader who knows it all and are more inclined to follow the egalitarian/participatory type of leadership. This is not only characteristic of Jamaica or the Caribbean but is a global phenomenon. As a generalization regarding the dimension of leadership, political culture in various countries and political culture globally is moving from relationships of deference to more egalitarian relationships requiring more participation and more mutual respect between leader and follower. If we understand this and apply it to our own experience then we begin to see a little more clearly why it is that leaders who cannot change from the old approaches are left behind, wondering why there are fewer and fewer followers, particularly among the younger age groups. Some leaders are set in their ways in requiring near absolute obedience and deference at the very same time that, for many reasons, the citizens and followers are much more in the mode of resistance to being directed and openness to being involved in an active leader–follower relationship.

NOTE

1. See Trevor Munroe, "Caribbean Thought and the Political Process", in *Contending With Destiny*, ed. Ken Hall and Denis Benn (Kingston: Ian Randle Publishers, 2000), 237–47.

3

CHANGES IN POLITICAL BEHAVIOUR AND POLITICAL CULTURE

In order to explain changes in political behaviour and political culture we need to understand the roles of social forces and of political socialization, which we discuss in chapter 4.

SOCIAL FACTORS AND FORCES

We can identify five important developments, or social factors, which have become very significant in the last 20 years.

The Rapid Rise in Levels of Education

The general level of education among most populations has risen extremely rapidly within the last decades. Fifty years ago in the Caribbean approximately 10 percent of the people had secondary education. In other words nine out of every ten did not have any secondary education. Fifty years later in some Caribbean states, such as Barbados and the Bahamas, 100 percent of the secondary-school age population has had some secondary education. In Jamaica and Trinidad and Tobago, seven out of ten of the secondary-school age population have had some secondary education.

In industrialized countries these figures are more dramatic. Education is very important because, generally, the less educated we are the more willing we are to defer to someone else. As a general rule the less educated a population the more deferential it tends to be and the more educated a population the less willing the individuals will be to simply accept what they are told to think, do or say.

Access to Information

We have often heard it said that we live in the information age. What this means simply is that information is coming to us from every direction, from all sorts of mechanisms, even when we may not be educated.

Therefore, more and more of the populations in the individual Caribbean territories as well as regionally and globally now have multiple sources of information available, which reduces their inclination to accept information from only one source. For example, among the least educated in formal terms in the Caribbean population, say on a sugar cane plantation or on a banana plantation, you would find that despite the relatively low level of education most have access to cable television. Many of them have travelled and are exposed to influences from abroad. Therefore, in contrast to 20 or 30 years ago, when many of them would never have questioned the leadership, these individuals are now able to say, "but I heard something different", or, "I have seen something else." This makes them less open to being ordered about and to following orders in the way that they may have been in earlier times.

Generally introduced in the Caribbean no more than 40 years ago, the radio became a general item in most homes. At the time of independence in Jamaica, television had just been introduced, and very few homes had a television set. Very small percentages of the population had access to television. Then came the telephone – land lines first of all and then cellular and, most recently, the Internet. Today also, cable television allows real-time, visual access to events taking place in any part of the world. The first war that was ever televised in real time by cable around the world was 10 years ago, the Gulf War. Therefore, the citizen in any part of the world in the year 2002 has access to information, has means of communication far greater than at any previous time in modern history. The more sources of information there are, the less dependent the population has to be on one source of authority.

In this context, it is interesting that Caribbean countries have a communication and information profile far above the rest of the developing world (see Table 3.1). For example, the average number of radios per thousand in 1995 in the Caribbean was about 620. The average for the developing world was 185 radios per 1,000 people. The Caribbean people are much more informed and have much more access to modern means of communication than elsewhere in the developing world. In one respect, the Caribbean is ahead of the industrialized world in terms of utilization of means of communication. We are ahead of the industrialized world and far above the global average in relation to international telephone calls. Table 3.1 shows that in the Caribbean the average time spent on international calls annually is 74 minutes per person. The average for all developing countries is 3 minutes, while the average for industrialized countries is 41 minutes. The Internet is the next phase of this revolution which will have a much greater social impact because what the use of the Internet does is to close the gap between experts in all kinds of areas and the ordinary person. For example, if you are suffering from diabetes you can learn so much about diabetes from

Table 3.1 Country Access to Information and Communication, 1995

Country	Radios[a]	TVs[a]	Telephones[a,c]	International Calls[b]	Cell Phones[a,c]	Internet[a]	PCs[a]
Barbados	900	287	437	123	111	5.4	57
Antigua & Barbuda	439	409	499	–	287	3.7	–
The Bahamas	735	233	376	–	104	2.0	–
Trinidad & Tobago	505	318	231	45	103	3.1	19.2
Dominica	634	141	294	–	16	1.2	–
St Kitts & Nevis	668	–	569	193	31	0.2	–
Grenada	598	158	332	82	46	0.1	–
St Vincent & the Grenadines	670	234	220	–	21	0.0	–
St Lucia	765	301	313	76	16	0.2	–
Jamaica	438	306	199	22	142	0.7	–
Guyana	494	42	79	24	46	0.1	–
Belize	587	167	149	27	70	2.3	28
Caribbean (average)	619	320	308	74	83	1.58	27.2
All developing countries (average)	185	145	78	3	52	0.5	6.5
Industrial countries (average)	1,005	524	524	41.6	459	18	156
World (average)	364	226	163	10.9	121	4.8	48.6

[a] Number per 1,000 people.
[b] Minutes per person.
[c] Data for 2000 from UNDP, *Human Development Report 2002* (New York: Oxford University Press, 2002), 186–89.

Internet Web sites that it narrows the gap between you and your doctor. This applies to any field of endeavour. To give an example related to political science, you can log on to a Web site that deals with information on Islam and you can soon learn more than I know in that particular area. This means that now we are as likely to be less naturally deferential, accepting all that we hear and see, because we now have greater capacity to evaluate things much more for ourselves than was possible in previous generations.

Population Movements

Population movements by way of travel, migration, and tourism have increased immensely in the last decades, due to the technological revolution in transportation, which has made it much cheaper and quicker to travel from place to place, from country to country, from region to region. The net effect of increased travel, migration, and tourism is greater exposure to different ideas, and to different ways of thinking and acting and an undermining of that which was considered traditional. More people are now seeing and experiencing directly what they may not even have heard about before.

Some of the most important leaders of change, not only in our region but elsewhere, have been persons who were exposed to other more modern ways of thinking and acting. For example, the first wave of migrants who left the Caribbean in the 1950s and went to England would for the first time have seen white people cleaning the streets and doing jobs they rarely did in the Caribbean. Think what this did to the traditional mental hierarchy brought about by the Caribbean social structure in which whites are at the top, browns are in the middle and blacks are at the bottom.

The powerful effect of travel, migration, and exposure to other cultures, which is now within the grasp of tens of millions more because of the cheapening of various forms of transportation, should not be underestimated. In that context, we should notice that in the Caribbean, not only does the largest percentage of the people live outside of the region but also that the people at the bottom of the social structure travel more compared to anywhere else.

Rapid Urbanization

Rapid urbanization means that fewer and fewer people are living in villages and districts of rural areas and more and more people are concentrated in cities. For example, in 1975, only about a quarter of the population of developing countries lived in urban areas. By 1998, that had changed to about 40 percent living in cities and urban concentrations.

Within that context, Jamaica is one of the most rapidly urbanizing countries in the entire hemisphere. Urbanization invariably means over-crowding. As the urban population expands more rapidly than the infrastructure, it means that there are inadequate housing, inadequate sewerage facilities and the growth of inner-city ghettos. This is a radicalizing influence, when people come to town from country expecting that it will be relatively easy to make good and discover that town is often harder than country. That is why this phenomenon of urbanization has carried with it everywhere a certain radicalization, of the youth in particular, and especially the unemployed or the underemployed youth. That radicalization of the young people in the adverse conditions of urbanization in turn generates a culture that reinforces the radicalization (for example through the phenomenon of inner-city music). That is one reason why Bob Marley's Trench Town music became not just a Jamaican phenomenon but the music grabbed the attention of so much of the world, where it resonated in the ghettos and with disadvantaged people around the world. One of the reasons for that is that the lyrics, the message, and the music spoke to the conditions of inner-city young people all over the world.

Opportunity Structure

In the last 10 to 15 years there have been increased inequalities in almost every single country. This means that in the last 10 to 15 years worldwide the way economies have been restructured and the way societies have reorganized have widened the gap between the few at the top and the majority in the middle and at the bottom. Consequently, the availability of opportunity for those at the base of the social pyramid has been negatively affected. As inequality has grown, so has dissatisfaction.

The inequality to which we refer is not just inequality within countries, but it is also an inequality based on other criteria, such as race and ethnicity so that the gap between black and white has widened globally. Gaps between different regions of the world have also widened and as people try unsuccessfully to close them, resentment grows. Resentment, envy, and discontent contribute to changes in the way people think and how they behave.

We conclude that as a result of a range of social forces affecting different countries, different regions, and different peoples to one degree or another, changes in attitudes and behaviour have been triggered. One of the changes that we see is that *dominant social ideologies* (the set of ideas that prevail in a particular country) begin to be radicalized because more and more the inherited structures and traditions are questioned, whether these are based on education, income, or religion. In that context we can think of Islam as one of the world's religions in which a section is becoming more radicalized from the main stream and is distorting and deforming the main stream message of Islam.

There are other sets of circumstances contributing to change. So far, we have examined the social factors. In chapter 4 we look more at the individual level, at the role of political socialization.

,

4

POLITICAL SOCIALIZATION

Political socialization may be defined as that process whereby society develops attitudes and feelings towards politics in each of its members. Political socialization, in other words, is political upbringing. Each of us has a political upbringing. Therefore, while we look at social causes in general we also need to look at our individual political upbringing – our individual political socialization. In looking at individual political socialization, we distinguish between two levels: primary and secondary.

PRIMARY POLITICAL SOCIALIZATION

Primary political socialization takes place through relationships or processes that are relatively informal, unstructured, and unorganized. The first agent is the *family* or, more broadly, the *household unit*. The family or household unit is extremely important in our political upbringing on at least two different levels. The first is that it is within the family that we are exposed for the first time to political loyalties and to political hostilities. Without knowing it, a child is able to sense where the loyalties of adults lie, which leader, which party they support or reject. This applies not only to political parties and political leaders but very early the household unit begins to pass on an attitude towards the country. The first exposure of the child to loyalty or unconcern or indifference is through the parents or guardian. This attachment is the first level in which political socialization operates within the family or household group.

The second level derives from the fact that the child is first exposed to authority and to power in the household. This exposure begins to form attitudes, responses to authority in general and not only household authority in particular. Attitudes of deference to authority within the household have implications for how the child deals with other authority. Therefore, we can immediately see what happens to primary political socialization if there is no authority at all in the household unit. If there is no authority at all, then there is no upbringing on how to deal with authority and invariably what that means is a rejection, a non-acceptance of any authority. We must understand how important the family and the household is to our individual political upbringing, not only to the child's political loyalties and hostilities but also to forming attitudes to authority. Hence the more families break down, the more authority in the home disappears. The more there is breakdown, erosion and decay, the more there will be children having children. The more parental authority is absent because the parent is compelled to work around the clock or to emigrate, the less socialization that each child experiences in how to relate to authority and how to manage authority. Globally family structures and household authorities are being eroded for many different reasons, so that political socialization in the home is being negatively affected.

The second primary agency of socialization is what we call the *peer group*. This is a group of individuals who frequently interact with each other. Usually members of a peer group share relatively equal status, and ties to one another are relatively close compared to ties to other people. Peer groups are clustered around a particular location. Increasingly peer groups can be found in the community, particularly in the inner-city community, and they are important sources of mutual reinforcement –in either negative or positive ways. The peer group socializes new members to conform to its ways of thinking and acting. It is a powerful source of political upbringing. The corner group or "crew", which can be found in inner-city communities in the Caribbean or anywhere else in the world, is a peer group with a big influence on collective behaviour and collective ways of relating to authority The gang is a very important peer group and to the extent that some gangs are more organized than others, they may also qualify as secondary sources of political socialization (described below).

SECONDARY POLITICAL SOCIALIZATION

Secondary political socialization takes place through mechanisms that are more formal, more structured, and more organized. The first agency is the *school* or *educational institution* (primary and secondary schools). These affect us politically in two different ways.

1. It is the first organized effort to inculcate or to transmit politically relevant consciousness, for example through teaching the national anthem, the symbolism of the national flag, the national pledge and national heroes. In every country in the world children begin to learn in the school system those symbols to which they are expected to attach themselves – symbols of nationhood, and of governmental and national authority. Of course, the

nature of that attachment and the extent of that transmission of political loyalties will vary from country to country. In that context, it is not irrelevant to note that the term Taliban (designation of the ruling authority in Afghanistan in the 1990s) comes from the word *talib* which means student. The Taliban got their name from schools in Pakistan for refugee children from neighbouring Afghanistan. Persons in that movement were inculcated with extreme Islamic views and loyalties in educational institutions set up in Pakistan with the mass migration from Afghanistan into Pakistan of millions of Afghan people. The young were put into schools where they were taught ideologies of hate, particularly against Western authority and any other authority that did not accept their extreme version of Islam.

2. The school is also our second exposure to authority. The schoolteacher, principal, and administrator are authorities to whom each child has to relate. How they relate to you as a child and you in turn relate to them as authority figures impacts on the development of your attitude towards authority.

The second agency is the *church* or other *religious institution*. In every society, religious beliefs and religious organizations play a significant role in socialization. Religion and the religious institution are more often than not the source of morality. It is the main origin of our ideas about right and about wrong because often religions have rules that define what is sin and what is virtue. For example, in countries that are predominantly Christian in their religious persuasion, the Ten Commandments are obviously the major set of rules defining what is right and what is wrong. Therefore, the success or otherwise of the religious institution is going to affect the attitudes or values of people in a particular country. In a predominantly Christian country where the church is effective, where it has a great impact, it will socialize people into the creeds of Christianity. It will socialize people to be their "brother's keeper" and it will socialize people into honesty. Conversely, where the church or Christian religion is ineffective people will not be effectively socialized into the creeds and the values of Christianity. This has an impact on politics, how people view politics and how people behave politically. If the church and religious teaching are effective, it means that the degree of corruption and the degree of dishonesty would likely be that much less.

Therefore, socialization by the religious institution is of importance in determining the values and attitudes as well as the behaviour of people, not just in religious terms but more broadly as well. This point becomes more important when the religious institution is part of the government. For example, in the states where the government upholds Islam, the religious institution not only becomes a source of political socialization but also a source of laws, and the origin of punishment. In Saudi Arabia, if you steal, it is not only a sin; it is also a crime for which the punishment is often to chop off your hand because it is their interpretation of the Koran (the holy book of Islam). If a woman commits adultery in Afghanistan, that woman, according to their interpretation of the Koran, can be stoned to death. The religious institution is not only a source of upbringing in terms of values but also where it is married to the state religion is also the source of law and punishment.

The third agency is the *mass media*: radio, television, newspapers, cinema, and, in more recent times, talk shows. Talk shows are very important in forming people's attitudes and influencing their values. As a result of the influence of popular talk shows, you are able to recite certain sayings from memory. One example is Wilmot Perkins' description of the politics of scarce benefits. Most of you can recite this by heart. He keeps saying it over and over and you keep hearing it over and over. Without your realizing it, this influences your attitudes even if you have not consciously analysed the statement and asked, "Is it appropriate or correct to some extent or is all of it correct?"

The fourth agency is the *political party*. Political parties in almost every country in the world today are major secondary institutions of political socialization, because in and through the political party the leadership tries to develop certain attitudes and to strengthen certain hostilities. The political party explicitly tries to socialize members to uphold and to support the party almost regardless of what it does.

When you look at the agents of socialization that we have identified, the primary ones first, then the secondary ones, you can begin to recognize that each one of us has been subjected to a political upbringing, even when we may not have been fully aware of it. Indeed, much of it takes place unconsciously.

In concluding, not all the socializing agencies have the same influences. Some are clearly more important than others. For example, in the world today the mass media is clearly a more influential socializing agency than the political party. One reason for this is that the media has much wider reach and political parties for many reasons no longer have the confidence and trust of the people as they did in the past.

To summarize, political culture and political behaviour are changing although aspects of them persist. These changes are occurring largely because of the impact of social forces and, at the individual level, because of political socialization.

THE CHANGING DEFINITION OF POLITICAL SCIENCE AND OF POLITICS

5

POLITICS AND THE NATURE OF POLITICAL SCIENCE

Your ideas of politics are determined not by your studies but by what you have seen and heard and associated with politics. Most of us equate politics with the stereotypical politician and because of this, most of us have the view that the nature of politics is power-hungry, self-seeking, corrupt, and, in some cases, violent. These ideas come from our socialization, as well as from our exposure to social forces and our own experiences with politicians. Therefore, it is understandable that this is the way in which we define politics.

However, that it is understandable does not mean that it is justifiable. It is no more justifiable to equate the nature of politics with corruption, self-seeking behaviour, violence, and power hunger than it is to equate the nature of Islam with terrorism. You cannot determine the nature of a phenomenon on the basis of how people who claim to practise it act. For example, how would we regard Christianity if we were to define Christianity on the basis on what has been done in the name of Christianity over the years? Remember that people were enslaved in the name of Christianity as a means of bringing civilization to them. We were told that we were colonized in the name of Christianity because we were inferior and we needed to be made superior by virtue of foreign rule. Nobody could reasonably define Christianity in terms of slavery and colonialism.

The nature of politics as we would consider it from our political socialization would lead us to define politics as anything that has to do with the government of a country – elections and so on. This definition is very similar to that found in the *Concise Oxford Dictionary* (ninth edition): "the art and science of government".

This short definition was thought to be acceptable for a very long time, and therefore two or three subjects were seen as making up political studies: the study of the constitution, constitutional law, and political philosophy. This definition has become inadequate from an academic point of view because of the developments and changes in political life described below, and because it narrows down the "political" to only a concern with government.

1. In the last 100 years there has been an expansion of the right to vote and in the number of people who have the right to vote. Up until 40 years ago in Jamaica only about 5 percent (that is, one in every twenty) had the right to vote. Similarly, in England it was only in 1928 that the right to vote was extended to everybody – Universal Adult Suffrage. In 1920, women got the right to vote in the United States. The development of mass voting led to interest and research in new branches of politics, such as the formation of public opinion, the study of voting behaviour, and political psychology.
2. Political parties became important as the main mechanism by which to organize the electorate. As these parties grew there arose the need to study them.
3. There was growth in the size and responsibility of government to include health, education, information, transportation, and communication. As government expanded, a bigger and more complex public administration, that is, the organization of civil service, became necessary. Public administration then became a subdiscipline of political science.
4. Interest groups or lobbies became organized to represent the interests of businesspeople, as well as professional groups such as teachers and doctors, and workers. One of the main purposes of these groups was to influence the policy of government to provide better conditions for the particular group. The study of interest groups is therefore important.
5. There is greater involvement of government in the economy. Before, government was very limited in size, scope, and power. Now, taxation, ownership of assets and utilities (telephone, electricity, water), and manipulation of the money supply (monetary policy) are major governmental concerns. This suggests the importance of studying political economy, or the relationship between the actions of government and the economy.
6. The great frequency of states dealing with one another and greater interaction between them underline the need for the study of international relations.
7. There has been a tremendous growth in the number of independent states – approximately 189 in 2000, compared with about 30 (the other states were colonies) 100 years ago. The rapid increase in the number of independent states encouraged investigation and comparison of political cultures and political/governmental structures, and therefore the development of comparative politics.

The idea of government and politics being defined solely as the art and science of government therefore became inadequate and the number of subjects grew from three – constitutional law, constitutional studies, and political philosophy – to include:

- Public opinion and voting behaviour
- Political psychology
- Public administration and public sector management
- The study of political parties and interest groups
- Political economy
- International relations
- Comparative politics

The nature of politics has expanded, and political science has become more complex, in keeping with the world in which we live.

There is a second sense in which the definition of politics as "the art and science of government" is inadequate. It is too formal; that is to say, it looks only at the structure of government, and therefore does not direct our attention to what is the essence of government behind the structure. When we look at the essence of government we discover what governments do, whatever they may be called. They make decisions, sometimes among conflicting opinions and options. No government operates without making such decisions, whatever its ideological label. For example, when the government finds the money to service the foreign debt instead of improving teachers' pay, a choice has been made.

Resources are limited, wants/needs are unlimited, and therefore choices have to be made. What this tells us therefore is that behind the structure and roles of government, the heart and soul of politics is decision making. Politics is not just the structure of government but the process of decision making – how decisions are made, what they are and how they are implemented. Clearly, the original definition is inadequate. If politics is the process of decision making then politics is everywhere.

Informal politics, for instance, is characterized by the presence of decision making, and of conflict, but the absence of government. There is no formal parliament, nor ministers, but there is politics, for example, in the family, in a relationship, in an office, in church – all of which we would be unable to study as politics were we to accept the dictionary definition.

The heart and soul of politics is not the prime minister or the electorate; these are part of the structure of national politics. The heart and soul of politics is decision making – choosing one thing against the other.

Decision making is also affected by the use of authority. Power and authority may look like the same, but they are not necessarily the same.

Power is the ability to get your own way, authority is the ability to get your way without the use of sanctions or threat thereof, but by virtue of a consensus that you have the right to do so. In other words, the legitimate right to do something is authority; the ability to impose sanctions is power.

Modern political science is the study of the process whereby binding decisions are taken. Second, it is the study of the decisions themselves and the nature of decisions taken. Third, it examines the impact of the decisions that are taken and considered binding by a given group. Hence, it is the study of the broad process, substance and impact of decision making – not just the art and science of government.

This leads us to look at the different levels of decision making with which political science is concerned. It is concerned, first of all, with decision making at the community level, the level of community activities. Second, it examines regional and local dimensions of decision making. This is a little broader in scope than looking at community activities, since the region takes in many communities. Third, it looks at the national level, the level of the country as a whole, such as Jamaica or Barbados. Fourth, political science considers the international level – the relationships (economic, cultural, diplomatic) between different countries.

DEMOCRACY: REPRESENTATIVE AND PARTICIPATORY; PARLIAMENTARY AND PRESIDENTIAL

6

THE STATE

The state is as central to politics and political science as the firm is to microeconomics or as social stratification is to sociology. The *state* may be defined as a set of institutions, offices and officials, whose decisions are regarded as binding over all and who have supreme authority to enforce compliance or obedience from the population of a given geographic area. We see from this definition that the state has both power and authority: it has the capacity to enforce and it has the right to enforce.

State power and state authority are divided into several different parts or branches:

1. Legislative power – the power to make laws.
2. Executive power – the power to administer or execute laws. This includes the public service or civil service bureaucracy.
3. Judicial power – the power to determine whether laws are broken and what punishments are to be inflicted. The judiciary is part of the criminal justice system, which also includes the security forces.

How the state is characterized is not determined by any one of these branches. The state has to be looked at as a whole or as a comprehensive system with different arms. When we are making a judgement about the character of a state, we have to look at the state in its totality. In addition, we need to distinguish between the state and the government. The state includes government but is larger and more complex than government. The government is responsible for the everyday guidance of the state but it is not the state. The government is that part of the state that is responsible for the coordination of policy but governments can and do change, whereas the state continues. The state, for example, includes the police, military, civil service, and machinery for tax collection. None of these changes when the government changes.

The state has the quality of supreme authority or sovereignty. The state has supreme authority over everything in its geographic boundaries but may not be the only authority. There are other authorities within any state, such as churches (having authority over its members), some with more authority than others.

Each state in the world today has sovereign or supreme authority but no state in 2002 has the same level of authority over its borders and the people in its geographic area as it did 30 years ago. In other words, while the quality of supreme authority remains, its effectiveness is being reduced, mainly by technological developments in the modern world, particularly the revolution in the technologies of information, communication, and transportation. No state today can prevent, in the way that it could in the past, its population from receiving ideas and images of which it disapproves. The ability of the state to control the movement of people is now significantly diminished. For example, as powerful as the United States is in terms of its military might and economic ability, it is impossible to have the same control in 2002 as in 1982 over the movement of people in and out of the country. In the year 2000, approximately 500 million people crossed the borders of the United States. It is almost impossible to search everyone at border checkpoints and to ensure that each person does not have biological, chemical, or other kinds of weapons that could be used for terrorist acts.

THE DRIVE TO INDEPENDENCE

In the second half of the twentieth century, around the world, groups of people rejected rule over them by other states. They wanted to have their own government, their own people ruling an independent state. As a result of this, the number of states has grown immensely.

In 1945, there were approximately 50 states in the world; in 2000 the membership of the United Nations, reflecting the number of states that have developed, is 189. This means that in the years since 1945, approximately 139 states came into existence, because people in different parts of the world were no longer content to have others ruling over them, they wanted to rule themselves. Among the states that emerged were the CARICOM states.

This drive for independence and statehood has not been without its problems. One of the problems of this issue of statehood is, when does a country qualify for independent statehood? What is it that makes 1 or 2 million people, or even fewer in some cases, qualify to have their own state? Some would answer that a group qualifies to have its own state on the basis of common history, common culture, common language, common economic community. The problem with this is twofold. What happens when there are a number of different cultures sharing the same history and sharing the same common geographic area? Which do you use to justify statehood – the culture, in which case you would have many different states, or the history, in which event you have one state?

There is also the issue of size. Is there is a lower limit below which a people cannot have a state, or below which a people do not have the resources or capacity to be independent? Because of the complexity of this issue, some people have voted recently against the general trend, and in favour of not having their own state. For example, in St Kitts and Nevis there were people in Nevis who felt that Nevis should be independent (the total population of St Kitts and Nevis is 50,000 to 60,000; the total population of Hanover, Jamaica, at the last count was 65,000). The movement for an independent Nevis was so strong that a referendum was held in 1999 and those who wanted independence for Nevis lost by a small minority.

In Puerto Rico, the people have voted repeatedly on the question of independence from the United States and, though with some complications, the majority has voted to remain part of the United States. Bermuda, with a population of approximately 60,000, voted some years ago to remain a colony of Britain. East Timor in Indonesia is an example of people who had to fight to gain independence. In Mexico, the people of one of the states of Mexico, Chiapas, felt that they wanted to be separated from Mexico. They revolted but were unsuccessful and still remain a part of Mexico.

Thus, the drive to independence and national statehood has been a powerful force in politics in the twentieth century, but it has not been universal. Some people have voted not to become independent; others have tried and have been suppressed by the larger political community to which they belong.

CLASSIFICATION

How do we classify states? The issue of classification of anything is, in a sense, arbitrary, in that classifications are neither right nor wrong but, rather, more or less useful. There are at least three ways to classify states in the modern world:

1. According to population size
2. According to history, economic structure, and economic organization
3. According to the source of authority

Population Size

States can be classified by population size into smaller states and larger states. By this method of classification, 45 percent of states in the modern world have populations of fewer than 5 million people. Normally, we associate smallness with a restricted ability to develop but this fact of smallness does not constitute an absolute obstacle to development in the modern world. Small states can and do develop, and have reached the peak of development in modern society. We may refer to the *Human Development Report*, published annually by the United Nations Develop Programme (UNDP), which ranks states according to their level of human development, as indicated by a combined measure of income, education, length of life, and quality of life. The 2001 *Human Development Report* indicated that a number of the top 30 states in the world in terms of human development are smaller states. Among the most developed states in the world in terms of human development are Norway (a little over 4 million people), Barbados (under 300,000), Singapore, Iceland, and Cyprus.

History, Economic Structure, and Economic Organization

When we use history, economic structure, and economic organization we come up with classification into first, second, and third world states. First world states are distinguished by the fact that they have not recently experienced colonial rule, that they have free market economies, and that they have a democratic political system. Second world states are those that broke away from the first world and established communist political systems and communist economic organizations. Third world states are those that have experienced colonial rule, where the economies were structured to meet the needs of the colonial power and the economies remain underdeveloped.

This classification is not as useful today as it was 30 years ago. In the first place, there cannot be a first, second, and third world when the second world has collapsed. Second, within the third world so many differences have emerged in terms of economic development and economic performance that, within the so-called third world, there are as many differences as common factors. For example, Singapore and Barbados, in terms of economic and human development, despite having experienced colonial rule, have more in common with developed countries than they do with countries such as Afghanistan or Bangladesh. How, then, can you justify classifying Barbados and Afghanistan as third world states? Although that classification remains in use, and while it is sometimes helpful, it is not as useful as it was in the past when there were fewer differences within the third world category and when, up until 15 years ago, there was still a second world in existence.

Source of Authority

States can be classified according to the source of authority or the location of power within the state. When we focus on that criterion for classification, we come up with two extremes. At one extreme, there are authoritarian or dictatorial states, sometimes called totalitarian states. At the other extreme when we use the criterion of location or concentration of power and authority, there are the democratic states.

7

AUTHORITARIAN STATES

An *authoritarian* state is one in which nearly total power is concentrated in an individual, a political party, the military, or a religious group. In this type of state there are certain characteristics regarding the rights of the people in relation to government and in relation to one another:

1. Elections in these countries, when they do take place, are neither fair nor free. They are rigged, to one degree or another.
2. There is either only one political party that has any real chance of holding state power or there is no political party because, as in the case of a military dictatorship, political parties are banned.
3. In these states, political rights are extremely restricted. By political rights, we mean the right, for example, to form a political party or the right to join a civic association. Most significantly, freedom of all kinds is severely restricted, including freedom of conscience (what you can think), freedom of speech, and freedom of the press. In a religious dictatorship, such as Afghanistan under the Taliban, not only is there no freedom of the media, but the people are denied access to the media (it is reported that citizen's television sets used to be destroyed under that regime).
4. In authoritarian states, there is a central role for the police, whether they act under religious direction or under some ideological direction. In Taliban Afghanistan, there was a Ministry of Vice and Virtue whose responsibility was to ensure that every one was virtuous according to the state's definition of virtue and to ensure that vice according to their definition was severely, and very often arbitrarily, punished.
5. In these states there is no equality in the rule of the law. The law is for some but the rulers are above the law. The rules that exist are influenced by the desires of the ruling group, which may change from time to time.

8

DEMOCRATIC STATES

In the modern world, approximately 60 percent of the states are classified as democracies. The word democracy comes from the bringing together of two Greek words, *demos*, which means people, and *kratia*, which means to rule. In democratic states, elections are relatively free and fair. One way of measuring whether elections are free and fair is the extent to which a state in its political history actually demonstrates that opposition parties do come to power by virtue of elections.

Consider an example of a state that claimed to be democratic but in which for 50 years, there were "free and fair" elections in which the same party was elected over and over. Then you would want to look at that state again to see whether those elections were really free and fair. On the contrary, if you consider a country in which there are claims of free and fair elections, in which oppositions kept getting elected and governments were removed by elections, then some democracy exists in that country, whatever weaknesses there may be.

In democratic states *political rights* are recognized and practised to some degree, for example the political right to organize into a party or the political right to form a student association or a trade union, as well as the political right to protest and to demonstrate. Of course, these rights are relative, because in every state there are rules governing the exercise of these rights, such as the conduct of protests and demonstrations. In addition to these political rights there are *civil liberties*, such as liberties of speech, freedom of the press, freedom to believe what you wish (freedom of conscience).

In a democratic state, political parties compete with each other and each has some reasonable prospect of winning the competition. However, the elected government is nevertheless limited in what it can do. It is limited by the constitution (the fundamental rules of the state) and by the laws of the country. A relatively independent judiciary enforces both the constitution and the laws, which operate to limit the government as well as set the framework within which the people function.

```
                                            ┌ Participatory democracy
                                   ┌────────┤
                                   │        └ Representative democracy
                  ┌────────────────┤
                  │                │
    Authoritarian         Democratic────────┐        ┌ Welfare state (Sweden)
                                             ├────────┤
    ┌──────┬──────────┬──────────┐          │        └ Minimalist state (US)
    │      │          │          │          │
 Military  Religious  Ideological            │        ┌ Presidential (US)
 (Pakistan (Taliban   (China)                └────────┼ Parliamentary (UK)
 Post-1999) Afghanistan)                              └ Semi-Presidential (France)
```

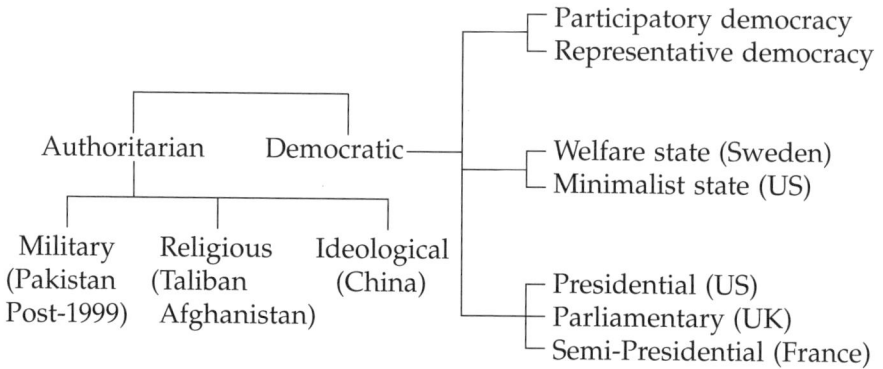

Figure 8.1   Diagram showing different types of states

Note that there is no totally authoritarian state, neither is there a totally democratic state. Each country is more or less close to being, but not purely, authoritarian or democratic. Each of these represents an extreme or pure type and neither exists in the real world. In an authoritarian state, although power is concentrated, control is never complete. For example, in slave society, obviously, power and authority were highly concentrated in the hands of the slave masters but that did not prevent the slaves from eluding the control of their masters. In the religious dictatorship prior to the removal of the Taliban government in Afghanistan, authoritarianism was not complete. There were areas that were not fully controlled and this allows us to say that a purely authoritarian state does not and in a way cannot exist, because it would be nearly impossible to fully control any human being.

In the same way, there is no pure democracy. Rights and freedoms are never absolute. We can distinguish two different periods in the life of a democratic state: normal times and extraordinary times or times of emergency.

In normal times, when life is more or less ordinary, with no emergency, the rights and freedoms in a democratic state are limited to some extent by law. For example, every democracy has some limitations on the right of free speech. There is no democracy in the world where you would be able to go into a crowded cinema and shout "fire" when there is no fire. You would immediately find that free speech is limited by the laws of public mischief. Many democracies limit free speech in relation to your ability to incite or stir up one section of the population to murder another. In Germany, today, preaching racial hatred is not allowed despite freedom of speech. Preaching hatred against white people or black people is not allowed because that country suffered greatly from the racialism of Hitler and his dictatorship. The military and the police in many democracies are not allowed to join trade unions or to go on strike. If they had that right, then it would endanger the rest of the society if it were exercised.

Extraordinary times or times of emergency may be brought on by war, against another country or against terrorism, or by a threat to public order due to extreme violent criminal activity. Times of emergency may also be brought on by a threat to public health. A recent example occurred in the democracy of Britain, where there was a threat to public health because of the spread of foot and mouth cattle disease. In those extraordinary times democracies everywhere preserve the legitimate right to limit freedoms in the interest of protecting the society.

For example, in the event of a threat to public order caused by extreme criminal violence, murder and other kinds of activity of that nature, any democratic state in the world remains a democracy even though it limits freedom of movement by way of curfew, requiring that no one in part of a city or in the entire city or, in the case of war, no one in the entire country is free to move about during certain hours. By definition, emergency conditions bring about emergency restrictions on freedoms and rights of various kinds. In some curfews where there is great danger, the security forces are given the right not just to intercept people but actually to shoot those who disobey the terms of the curfew. On many occasions in the United States when curfews were imposed, perhaps because of a riot and looting, security forces were given the right to shoot any one found moving around the streets during the period of curfew. In other words, the rights that are normal have abnormal limitations in order to protect the society as a whole.

The main right now being debated in most democracies around the world, including Jamaica, is the right to privacy and personal freedom (and how to legitimately limit this right in the context of the war against terrorism). This is a normal right. Everyone has a right to privacy in their homes when using the telephone. But this right everywhere is being examined to see how can it be restricted in order to allow the telephone calls of suspected criminals or suspected terrorists to be intercepted in order to prevent or reduce the likelihood of criminal activity or terrorism endangering the whole society.

Limiting of freedoms in this manner does not necessarily diminish the extent to which a state is a democracy. In relation to democracy there are two factors to consider: first, restrictions in normal times have to be very limited if the country is to remain a democracy. Second, the restrictions imposed in extraordinary times have to be temporary. An indefinite curfew would begin to bring into question whether that country was a democracy.

States can and often do change from one type to another. In other words, a state may be authoritarian at a particular point in time but at a later point becomes democratic. Conversely, a state can be democratic at a certain point in time, and become authoritarian or dictatorial. For

example, in 1994, South Africa was clearly and unambiguously an authoritarian, dictatorial state based on racial exclusivity. The white racial minority had the rights while the black majority had none. In the year 1996,
South Africa made the transition from being an authoritarian state to
being a more democratic state with the abolition of many restrictions on
the rights of blacks, including the right to vote and other rights of various
kinds being conceded after a long period of struggle. A converse example
is Pakistan (South-East Asia), which up to 1998 was more or less a
democratic state. However, in October 1999, there was a military coup
and the military took power, abolished the right to vote and other such
rights and therefore, in 2002, Pakistan has become a more authoritarian
and dictatorial state led by General Musharraf.

What this means for us as students of political science is that it
imposes an obligation on us to determine where a state is at any particular point in time, not by looking at one indicator but by looking at many
indicators. A political scientist ought not to determine that a state is
democratic or undemocratic only by looking at elections in that state. A
number of issues should be examined, including elections, political rights
such as the right to form associations and to organize parties, freedom
of speech, freedom of conscience, and the extent of the rule of law. When
these are looked at together, it is then possible to come to a conclusion
regarding the health of that particular democratic state.

Democratic states are in the vast majority in the modern world. Therefore, the question arises, are all democratic states the same or are there
differences? While democratic states have in common the recognition of
the rights and freedoms described above, there are nevertheless sub-
types of democracy. Distinctions need to be made within the category of
democracy in examining the nature and character of democratic states.

9

TYPES OF DEMOCRACY

DIRECT AND INDIRECT DEMOCRACY

Direct and indirect democracy may be distinguished according to how the people exercise their power or their rule in the democratic state. However, as with authoritarian and democratic states, these types do not exist in pure form.

Direct Democracy

A *direct democracy*, sometimes called a participatory democracy, is a state in which the people themselves play a more direct role in running the state, in making laws and taking decisions. The country that most typifies a direct or participatory democracy is the small European state of Switzerland. Switzerland is about three times the size of Jamaica in terms of population and almost four times in terms of area. In Switzerland, consistent with being a more direct or participatory democracy, most of the important decisions are taken not by elected representatives but by the people themselves voting on issues in what is called a referendum. For example, in 1992, when Switzerland was considering whether to join the International Monetary Fund and the World Bank, the decision was not made by the elected representatives, but by putting it to all the people in a referendum. In 2000, the issue arose in Switzerland, like in many other European countries, as to whether to limit the number of foreign workers. That decision was not made by the elected officials; again this issue was put to the people, the majority of whom voted not to limit the number of foreign workers coming to Switzerland to seek employment and to explore opportunity.

These are two examples of what it means for a country to be a more participatory democracy. Important decisions are made by the people themselves and the state provides institutional means whereby the people can exercise their right to decide. The referendum is one such mechanism. Another example is the right of recall, which gives the people the legal means of terminating the tenure in office of any elected official before his or her term is up. In other words, if the members of Parliament or elected representatives are elected for five years, where the right of recall does not exist a member can be in office for five years regardless of how he or she performs. Where the right of recall does exist, during the five-year period the people are able to intervene directly. A certain percentage of the electorate in the constituency that elected that official can raise the issue of whether the person should be allowed to continue, either because the official is incompetent, inefficient, or has not kept campaign promises. The right of recall exists in about 12 states in the United States.

Indirect Democracy

An *indirect or representative democratic state* is one in which the people play a limited role in making decisions, such as in the passing of laws, between elections. Between elections the politicians rule, not in any absolute sense because they too have limitations, but they have a more active and direct role than the people.

Increasingly, in indirect democracies, there is a modern tendency for the use of the referendum to make decisions on certain issues. For example, Jamaica in 1961 was to decide whether to remain within the West Indian Federation. The decision was made by the people in a vote and the majority of the people voted to withdraw from the federation. In the United Kingdom in 1997 the decision needed to be made as to whether the electoral system should be changed in Scotland and Wales. This decision could have been made by the government but it was made by referendum. The people were asked and they voted for a change in the electoral system for both Scotland and Wales.

Indirect democracies use referendums to decide issues of three types:

1. When the issue relates to a fundamental structure of the state, which may be the electoral system or the boundaries of the state. For example, in Canada, the decision was to be made as to whether Quebec (one of the provinces of Canada) should become independent or remain a part of the Canadian Federation. Because this related to a fundamental structural question the decision was made by the people. The people of Quebec voted by a very narrow majority to remain in the Canadian Federation.
2. When the issue is controversial in so far as the people and/or their political leaders are divided on the issue. In that context, rather than the political leadership taking the decision, increasingly the matter is put to the vote in a referendum for the people themselves to decide.

3. When issues relate to moral questions. For example in many European states, particularly those that are predominantly Roman Catholic, the issue of abortion is a very controversial one and in a number of cases that issue was determined not by elected representatives but by the people themselves voting in a referendum. Similarly, in a number of states in the United States, the controversial issue of whether ganja should be decriminalized or legalized, either totally or for specific purposes, was not decided by the elected representatives but by the people. In some states the people have voted that it should be legal to prescribe ganja for medicinal purposes.

There are strong arguments for and against the more frequent use of referendums in indirect democracies.

- Argument for the use of referendums: If democracy means the people rule and if the people today are more informed and have less confidence in their political leadership, then clearly to ensure that decisions are accepted by the people it is best for the people themselves to decide.
- Argument against the use of referendums: When an election is held, a government is elected to rule. The government is elected not only to decide easy issues but in order also to make tough decisions. Therefore, for an elected government to go back to the people on issues is to undermine the legitimacy of government.

WELFARE AND MINIMALIST STATES

There are other ways of distinguishing different types of democracy. One relates to the position of the "free market" or the position of the private sector compared to the state in a democracy. This position varies and allows us to make another type of distinction among democracies based on that criterion. The distinction is between the welfare state and the minimalist state. In a welfare state the market and the government have a different relationship to one another than that between the market and the government in a minimalist state.

In the *welfare state* the government and the public sector play a big and active role in the economy and the society. Government and the public sector play a role as owner of means of production. Not only do they own public utilities, in some cases they own enterprises of one sort or another, airlines for example. In addition to being owners, the state is also a provider of social insurance, such as unemployment benefits and a national health service. The welfare state also acts as a regulator and provides the framework for the market to operate.

In contrast, in a *minimalist state* the government owns little or nothing. The government provides little and restricts its activity and responsibility primarily to being a facilitator of private enterprise and of market activities and to ensuring basic requirements, such as law and order and education.

Welfare States

The best examples of welfare states are in Northern Europe, particularly Sweden and Denmark. In this type of state a significant proportion of national resources is spent on social security, including pension benefits. In these democracies, the primary concern is with equality. That is to say, the gap between the top and the bottom should not be too wide and there should be a minimum below which no one should fall. In welfare states, in order to pay for these benefits, taxation tends to be higher, particularly on the better-off section of the population. Those with higher incomes are taxed significantly more heavily than those with lower incomes. From those levels of taxation, the government or the state finances the welfare benefits.

Minimalist State

Minimalist states are sometimes called free market states because the market is free to develop the economy, and provides welfare to those who can pay for it while the government does the minimum in terms of providing welfare services. The best example of this is the United States. The emphasis, in contrast to the welfare state, is on freedom. Usually in the minimalist state the levels of taxation tend to be lower than in the welfare state, because the government does not require the revenue to fund substantial welfare provisions. In Sweden, about 18 percent of the gross domestic product (GDP) is spent on social security benefits. In the United States, about 7 percent of GDP is spent on social security benefits.

The welfare state was predominant throughout the world in one form or another in the 50 years between 1930 and 1980. The minimalist state was predominant prior to 1930 and is again predominant subsequent to 1980.

PRESIDENTIAL DEMOCRACY AND THE PARLIAMENTARY DEMOCRACY

Presidential and parliamentary democracies are distinguished from each other on the basis of the ways in which the main branches of state power are connected to or disconnected from one another. Let us recall the three main branches of state power:

1. The legislative branch makes laws binding on the population over which the state exercises sovereignty.
2. The executive branch has the responsibility for making policies and of putting the laws into effect.
3. The judicial branch, sometimes called the judiciary, functions to enforce laws, make judgements when laws are broken, and impose punishments and sanctions when there are infringements.

Presidential Democracy

In a presidential democracy the main branches and institutions of the state are separated from one another, hence in the literature you will see that one of the principles of the presidential type of democracy is the "separation of powers". This principle refers to the fact that in this type of state each of the powers (executive, legislative, and judicial) is separate from the other two. Second, even though they are separate from one another each power is able to check, or limit, the power of the others. Hence, you will see that the second principle of the presidential type of state is "checks and balances".

In this type of democracy, therefore, the electorate elects directly two branches of the state power: the legislative branch and the executive branch. The electorate has two agents whom it chooses to watch over each other, with neither one being more powerful than the other and each separate from the other, thus balancing the power between them, as shown in Figure 9.1.

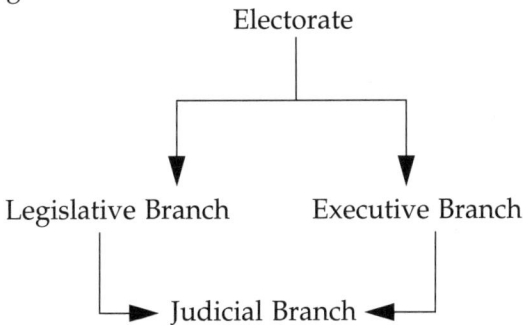

Figure 9.1 Diagram showing different branches of presidential democracy

This type of democracy predominates in South America or Latin America and in parts of South-East Asia. The original model of the presidential type of democracy is the United States. The strength of this system is that it is very difficult, though possible, for one section of the state to dominate and dictate because the power is divided and each branch is supposed to be equal to the other.

Parliamentary Democracy

In the parliamentary type of democracy, the main branches, in particular the legislature and the executive, are more combined than separated, in the sense that the executive is chosen from among the members of the legislature. The members of the executive come from the legislature, are members of the legislature at the same time and are responsible to the legislature. In this type of democracy (as shown in Figure 9.2) the electorate really chooses one agent – the legislature – whereas in the presidential type the electorate chooses two agents – the legislature and the executive.

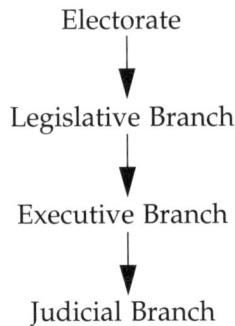

Electorate

Legislative Branch

Executive Branch

Judicial Branch

Figure 9.2 Diagram showing different branches of parliamentary democracy

Most presidential systems are republics but not all republics are presidential democracies. There are parliamentary systems where the head of state is called a president. What determines the nature of the system is not the name given to the head of state but the relationships among the electorate, the legislature, the executive, and the judiciary. For example, Trinidad and Tobago is a republic although it has a parliamentary system. The head of state in Trinidad and Tobago is a president.

The main strength of the parliamentary system is that in normal times the executive branch of the government can get things done. In other words, it commands the majority of the legislature and therefore can usually get the support of the legislature.

Main Weaknesses of the Presidential and Parliamentary Systems

The Presidential System

Sometimes there is stalemate in this system. This happens when the power is so balanced that the neither the legislature nor the executive can carry a majority decision.

The Parliamentary System

Sometimes the executive, and in particular the prime minister, is so dominant, because his or her majority of the legislature is so large, that the prime minister can do as he or she wishes – a "prime ministerial dictatorship".

There are slightly more presidential systems than parliamentary systems among democracies. The parliamentary type of democracy is predominant in western Europe and the Caribbean, whereas the presidential type is predominant in South America and South-East Asia.

The Semi-Presidential System

There is a third type of democracy, called a *semi-presidential system* because it has elements of both the presidential and parliamentary systems. Examples of this are France, Russia, and, in the third world, Sri Lanka.

The distinguishing feature of the semi-presidential system is that the executive has Both a prime minister and a president. The president is directly elected by the people – to this extent the system is similar to the presidential system. The people also elect the legislature, which then appoints a prime minister from among the members of the legislature. The prime minister remains in that position as long as he or she has the majority support of the legislature and therefore to this extent it is similar to the parliamentary system. The semi-presidential system has a dual executive and it is important for the prime minister to have the confidence of the legislature as well as the president. When the roles of the president and prime minister are not clearly defined or when there are differences between them conflict results.

SUMMARY

We have defined what a state is and we looked at the various ways of classifying states. We classified them in terms of size and population; then into first world, second world, and third world; and by the concentration and dispersion of power.

We said that there were two ideal types with regard to the concentration of power: authoritarian (dictatorial or totalitarian) states and democratic states. In the real world, states differ in degrees much more than they differ in kind; most states fall somewhere between these two extremes. We classified democratic states into representative and participatory democracies and we looked at the differences among states depending on the nature and role of the market in relation to the public sector. In this context, we saw that there were welfare states and minimalist states, sometimes called free-market democracies because the market plays such an extraordinary role. We broadly identified the ways in which the presidential and parliamentary types of democracy differed from each other, and we described a semi-presidential type, which has characteristics of both.

THE PRESIDENTIAL AND PARLIAMENTARY SYSTEMS OF GOVERNMENT

10

THE AMERICAN PRESIDENTIAL SYSTEM AND THE BRITISH PARLIAMENTARY SYSTEM

To begin this comparison we must recall how each of these democracies originated because, by and large, how a phenomenon, an organism or a type of state begins greatly influences the course of its development. It is very important to remember that the United States was born in a revolutionary war against British colonial power. Therefore, you would expect that a state established out of a revolution would break with the past. We should also remember not only that the United States was born in a revolutionary war against British colonial power but also that the war was led by relatively successful people. It was guided and led by financially successful planters who owned thousands of acres of land, by successful merchants and successful lawyers. A large percentage of these men were also slave owners. Therefore, in carrying out the revolution they were concerned with two things: first, to get rid of the British colonial power and, second, that the system they set up did not allow the slaves and the poorer people, the labourers and small farmers, to overturn them. It was a revolution pointing both against colonial rule and popular uprising, not least of all because at the time there were many signs that the labourers, small farmers, and slaves were themselves restive. The revolution aimed to remove foreign colonial rule while safe-guarding against popularly controlled government.

A new state was established with a new constitution in 1789. There-fore, the American Constitution and the American state legitimately claim the distinction of being the oldest constitutional democracy.

The British state by contrast was not established by revolution. British parliamentary democracy developed as a result of evolution, of gradual change, and not from the overthrow of a previously existing system. Therefore in Britain, the rule of the king was not overthrown the way it was in the United States. The rule of the monarch and aristocracy was gradually undermined over a number of centuries. The gradual nature of the change meant that the old structures and institutions were never cast aside. There was a king or queen 500 years ago; today there is a queen. However, while the structures and institutions remained, their functions and their powers were significantly changed. Therefore, the king of 1500 had immense, almost total, power but today the monarch has little power and her role is mainly symbolic. Because of evolution other old institutions remain, but with different roles and authority.

These contrasting origins have a number of implications for American presidential democracy and British parliamentary democracy.

1. The American structure of government, because it was new and revolutionary, had to be set down in one document, called the Constitution of the United States. We therefore say that the US Constitution is *codified*. In contrast the British structure of government is not set out or embodied in any single document. British parliamentary democracy is based on a number of laws passed over many years, indeed over many centuries. It is also made up of conventions, traditions, and customs of governance changing over time and passed down from one generation to another. Therefore, you will read in many of the writings on the American presidential and British parliamentary systems that the US Constitution is written and the British Constitution is not. This is generally speaking true but not as precise as it should be. The difference is not that one is written and the other is not, the difference is that the US Constitution is codified in one document whereas the British Constitution is written in a number of different documents.

2. There is a difference in political culture. We saw how important the values, attitudes, and beliefs are of any particular people in understanding how the government and the political process work. In the United States, there is great distrust of the power of government. One reason is that their democracy originated from revolt against the oppressive power of a colonial authoritarian state. Distrust for government is one of the great unifying values in American political culture. Related to this feature of the political culture is the great emphasis on individual freedoms. Individual rights in that culture must to a large degree prevail even against majority opinion. British political culture, in contrast, has a considerable respect for tradition, a respect for customs handed down from generation to generation. There is a greater regard for authority because authority in their history has not been regarded as being particularly oppressive. In fact, authority has been willing, under pressure, to change with time and hence, respect for position, authority, and custom remains relatively strong. Similarly, and for the same reason, there is a regard for inherited institutions. If you were to do a

poll in Britain today you would probably find that the majority of people are in support of the monarchy, because the monarchy as an inherited structure has demonstrated a capacity to change with the times. It has not been rigid, inflexible and in need of being cast aside. The Americans, unlike the British, show great irreverence for hierarchy and titles.

The origin of these two classical, typical democracies has a great deal to do with how the framework of the state was set and how the values of the people evolved in the context of democracy. Against this background we can look at structures.

THE LEGISLATURE

The United States is a federal state, whereas Britain is a unitary state. A federal state is one in which there are is a "central" state authority and there are state authorities in various geographic regions. Each of these groups has independent areas of jurisdiction and each has autonomy. The United States is constituted of 50 regional or geographically based states and a federal government based in Washington, DC. Each of the states has power over their own area. Thus, the State of Florida has its own executive (headed by the governor of Florida), legislature, and court system. Alongside this is the federal government, with the president and other offices.

The distrust of power and of too much power or authority residing in the hands of one body or individual is reflected in how the American states were set up, to ensure that there was no one state power. Instead there is a federal system in which, in addition to the federal state, different powers are held by the various states that constitute the union.

The division between the power of the state and the power of federal government and where the line is to be drawn has been a real issue in American democracy. For example, in the US presidential elections of 2000, the State of Florida, through the Florida Supreme Court, ruled that the counting of ballots for the presidential candidates should continue, but the Supreme Court of the United States ruled that the counting of the ballots should end. There remains a huge debate as to whether the Supreme Court of the United States exceeded its power by imposing its point of view on Florida and overruling the Supreme Court of Florida.

A federal state or federation is one in which there is central government along with regional governments, each with their own autonomy, structures, and systems. In 1959 and 1960 for example, Jamaica was a member of the West Indies Federation. There was a federal government for all the islands based in Port of Spain, Trinidad, alongside island governments, each with its own jurisdiction.

In a unitary state, power resides in the central government, which delegates or devolves some of its power to regions or to local government. That power is *not derived from an independent source*. The US Constitution sets out that each state has autonomy, whereas in Britain each region (Scotland, Wales, Northern Ireland) has regional power that is derived from London. This power can be taken away by London because Britain is a unitary state.

In a unitary state (of which Jamaica is an example) there is, for example, one police force. In a federal system there are many police forces. For example, there is a Florida state police, which is different from the Federal Bureau of Investigation. In contrast Jamaica has only one constabulary force for the entire island.

LEGISLATIVE STRUCTURE IN THE UNITED STATES AND BRITAIN

US legislative power is set out in Article 1 of the Constitution, which states that legislative power resides in Congress. Congress is composed of two different chambers or houses: the House of Representatives, with 435 members, and the Senate, with 100 members. The British legislature, which is called Parliament, also has two chambers: the House of Commons, with 659 members, and the House of Lords.

In both legislatures, there are a number of committees. In the United States Senate and the House of Representatives there are between 20 and 30 committees each. In the British Parliament there are also committees in the House of Lords and the House of Commons. However, we note one important difference. In the American Congress, the committees are extremely powerful, whereas the committees in the British Parliament are weak in comparison. The committees in the American Congress are very powerful for a number of reasons: (1) No proposal can become a law unless it is approved by the relevant committees in both houses of Congress. Any proposal before becoming law must be debated and approved in committee, and then voted on by the entire Senate and House of Representatives. (2) The American Congressional committees have power of investigation to probe issues affecting any aspect of American society or government, and the authority to summon anyone in the United States to testify. In Britain many proposals of law can be passed without going to a committee. That could not happen in the United States.

Election of Members of Congress

The members of both houses are elected by universal adult suffrage (every citizen over the age of 18 has the right to vote). The Senate has 100 members, 2 from each state. Alaska, with the smallest population, has 2 senators and California, with the largest population, is also represented by 2 senators. This is intended to reflect the equality of the states in a federation regardless of size and population. Each senator is elected for six years.

In contrast to the Senate, in the House of Representatives, the number of representatives from each state varies according to the population. For example, California, the most populous state, has 42 representatives, whereas Alaska, the least populous, has 1. Each member of the House of Representatives is elected for two years.

The Founding Fathers of the Constitution devised a scheme in which each senator is elected for six years but not all come up for election at the same time. Every two years a third of the Senate is up for election. This is called a staggered system. One reason for this is that the makers of the Constitution wanted to ensure that the people could not change the entire legislature at once. This is a brake against popular power.

The staggered elections to the Senate reveal what is part of the culture of the United States, the distrust of power, whether that power is an absolute monarch, which they overthrew, or the power of the majority. Power concentrated in any one institution increases the risk of abuse of power, hence the staggering of elections to the Senate.

Two political parties have been dominant in both the House of Representatives and in the Senate over the years. In 2002, the majority of the House of Representatives are members of the Republican Party, following the elections of November 2000. In the Senate, the situation is different, as the majority belongs to the Democratic Party: there are 50 democrats, 1 independent member, and the minority of 49 belongs to the Republican Party. Note that one of the features of the presidential system is that the majority of the legislature can be of a different party than that of the president or the executive. In this case Democrats are the Senate majority, whereas the president is a Republican.

Structure of the British Parliament

The British legislature, or Parliament, has three elements: the House of Lords, the House of Commons, and the monarch. The presence of the monarch as a formal member of each of the two chambers of the legislature indicates that in form the institutions have remained the same. The monarch was a member of the House of Lords and presided over the House of Commons 500 years ago and so it is today. The difference is that in the year 2002 the monarch has little or no power and the position is almost entirely ceremonial. The position remains but the power has been totally. changed.

In the House of Lords, there are three parts. The first is constituted of persons who are members on the basis of heredity: those who were born into an aristocratic family are entitled to a seat. These titles are passed down from generation to generation. Up until November of 1999, those who were members of the House of Lords by virtue of birth numbered more than 700. Therefore, they were the majority of the House of Lords. However, a process of constitutional reform has been taking place and in the last three to four years this has changed drastically in that after November 1999 all but 90 of the hereditary positions were abolished from membership in the House of Lords.

The second part of the House of Lords is appointed by the prime minister. The prime minister in the United Kingdom has the power to appoint persons to membership in the House of Lords by giving them titles. For example, Margaret Thatcher, after removal from office as prime minister, was given a title – Lady Margaret Thatcher – and, by virtue of being given a title by the prime minister who succeeded her, she sits in the House of Lords.

The third part is made up of persons who sit by virtue of the official positions they occupy, mainly in the church and in the judiciary. For example, all the leading bishops of the Anglican Church in the United Kingdom are members of the House of Lords.

The House of Lords is a very curious combination of tradition surviving over many centuries and a degree of modernity recently legislated. The House of Lords, by its composition, undermines the democratic principle because the members are not elected by the people. This is very much in contrast to the United States Senate, in which each senator is elected by the people. Consistent with this observation, the House of Lords has relatively insignificant power compared with the United States Senate. In the American system, laws cannot be passed without the approval of the Senate. The British House of Lords, by contrast, has the power to delay but not prevent a law from being passed. It has the power to delay passage of a law by asking the House of Commons to examine amendments that they may propose, but after that the House of Commons may proceed to pass the law. This reflects the idea that, because the members of the House of Lords are not elected, they should not be able to prevent legislation proposed by those who are elected.

The House of Commons, the second chamber in the British Legislature, is the elected house and it has 659 members. Each member represents a particular constituency and is elected for a maximum of five years. It should be noted that the date of elections, in particular to the House of Commons, is not fixed and can and does vary within the five-year term. The date on which the election is held is determined by the prime minister. The ability of the prime minister to determine the date of the election and to set that date at any point within the five years is dramatically demonstrated in the Caribbean version of the parliamentary system in Trinidad and Tobago. There, elections were held in December 2000 and again in December 2001. In the United States, the president does not set the date of an election. This is fixed by the Constitution.

In the British House of Commons two major parties, the British Labour Party and the Conservative Party have dominated representation. However, there has been consistent representation by third and minority parties. Thus, it is not strictly accurate to say the British system is a two-party system. It is more accurate to say it is a two-and-a-half-party system because of the consistent representation by minority parties. In that regard, the main minority party, the Liberal-Democrats has consistently received between 15 percent and 20 percent of the electorate vote but because of the electoral system their representation in the House of Commons has been far below the proportion of the population voting for them. Although 15 percent to 20 percent of the electors vote for a third party the number of seats won is in the region of 5 percent to 7 percent. The reason for this is the nature of the electoral system, which is called a "first past the post" system. This electoral system biases representation against minority parties by giving them disproportionately less representation and biases representation in favour of majority parties. This is so in England as well as in the Caribbean community. It has been very difficult for third or minority parties to achieve the level of representation consistent with their popular standing.

Finally, in contrast to the American Congress, voting in the House of Commons is very much according to party affiliation, albeit not exclusively.

THE EXECUTIVE

The United States

In the United States, the executive power is identified in Article 2 of the Constitution, which specifies that the executive shall be a president. The president is elected on a fixed date every four years, that is, "the first Tuesday, after the first Monday in November every four years". The president is elected by a system that combines direct election with indirect election by the people.

When the Constitution was being drafted in the 1780s, there was disagreement between those who wanted the people and the people alone to elect the president and supporters of the other point of view, that the president should be chosen by Congress. Eventually, what was decided was a compromise. The people should vote for the president but the final outcome should not rest with that popular vote; the final determination should rest with an electoral college. For example, the popular vote, the choice of the majority who voted in November 2000, was for the candidate of the Democratic Party, Al Gore, but the electoral college, by virtue of how it is constituted, voted for the Republican Party candidate, George W. Bush. This only happened once before in US history, in 1888.

The electoral college has 538 members, or electors, the same number as there are members of Congress (100 senators and 435 representatives), in addition to three members representing the District of Columbia. Thus, the electoral college allows each state membership equivalent to the number of its representatives in Congress. For example, the State of Florida has 25 members in the electoral college, which is equivalent to 23 members in the House of Representatives plus 2 senators.

In the presidential election, the members of the electoral college vote in accordance with a "winner take all" system. For example, in the November 2000 election, in the State of Florida, the people voted 51 percent for George W. Bush and 49 percent for Al Gore. Under the winner take all system, therefore, all 25 electoral college votes from that state went to George W. Bush. Even though he got the popular vote by a small margin he received all the electoral college votes. In this system, it is possible for a candidate to get the popular vote in the most populous states, California and New York for example, but lose in a majority of the states. Thus, in our example, Al Gore won the majority of votes in 14 of the states and George W. Bush won a majority in 36 of the smaller states. However, Al Gore won the popular vote by 400,000 votes. When the electoral college voted there were 271 for George W. Bush and 267 for Al Gore. A simple example will illustrate.

States	No. of Votes	No. of Electoral College Members	Popular Votes	
			Candidate 1	Candidate 2
A	1,000	50	800	200
B	500	25	100	400
C	300	20	100	200
D	200	10	99	101
Total	2,000	105	1,099	901

Electoral College Votes

States	Candidate 1	Candidate 2
A	50	0
B	0	25
C	0	20
D	0	10
Total	50	55

Figure 10.1   The US Electoral College and the popular vote for president

In our example candidate 1 won the popular vote by virtue of winning the most populous state A by a big majority, but candidate 2 won the electoral college vote by virtue of winning majorities in a number of states. Candidate 2 would therefore become president. This system restrains the power of the people by interposing an electoral college between the popular vote and the election of the president.

The only function of the electoral college is to elect the president. It meets on December 18 after the November election in each of the 50 state capitals and the District of Columbia and once it has voted it ceases it exist. The only purpose of the electoral college is to cast the vote for president in keeping with the majority vote in each state. It is not a permanent structure of the US governmental system.

The president holds office for four years. Amendment 22 to the Constitution (passed in 1951) limits the number of terms a president can serve to two terms, or eight years.

The president has considerable power, in a number of different dimensions of the state: first, as commander in chief of the armed forces; second, as the chief diplomat; and third, in initiating policies and legislation. However, in each of these roles, and in others as well, the authority of the president is checked and balanced by other branches of the presidential system. For example, the president as commander in chief has the constitutional authority to deploy US troops, but the president does not have the authority to declare war on another country. The Congress is the only body that has the authority to declare war. The difference between sending troops and declaring war is a technical difference which may be important in law, but in practical terms does not have great significance because the dispatch of troops can be in effect a declaration of war even though the Congress has not formally declared war. The Founding Fathers ensured that the power was divided and not concentrated. Another example relates to the president's Cabinet or chief advisers. The president is authorized to nominate persons to his Cabinet (for example, Secretary of State Colin Powell). Each nominee, however, is subject to confirmation or rejection by the Senate.

Once elected the American president can only be removed by three circumstances: death, resignation, or impeachment and conviction. It is important to note that there have been presidents in the history of the United States who have been removed in each of these three circumstances.

For example, in the 1960s President Kennedy was removed by assassination and was succeeded by the vice president. President Nixon resigned in 1974 in order to avoid impeachment and conviction. Once in the nineteenth century a president was impeached and convicted, and it almost happened in 1999 when President Clinton was impeached. In the case of an impeachment the Senate becomes the jury and votes to determine if the president is to be convicted. President Clinton was impeached on two charges, perjury and obstruction of justice. When the Senate voted in February 1999, 55 were in favour of conviction and 45 against on the perjury charge and 50 voted in favour and 50 against conviction on the charge of obstruction of justice. In order to convict a president the Senate must vote for conviction by a two thirds majority, or at least 67 votes.

The position of president is an extremely powerful one, but that power is limited in the United States by separation of powers and a system of checks and balances. Because it is possible for the majority in Congress to be of the opposing party, the president may find his or her proposal blocked by either house. For example, between 2000 and 2002 the president did not control the majority in the Senate, though he had the majority in the House of Representatives.

In the last 20 to 30 years, the American people have more often than not elected for president someone of a different party from the majority of those they elect to either or both houses of the Congress. Again, this reflects the political culture. It could be concluded from the way the American people vote that they do not want the same party to constitute the executive and the majority in the Senate and in the House of Representatives. This kind of "divided government" demands a lot of compromise. A president's term of office does not depend on controlling a majority of the legislature. In addition, a member of the president's party in the legislature can vote against the president without the fear that by so doing he or she will bring down the government. The president cannot call an early election nor can the legislature vote out the president except by impeachment and conviction. Each is independent of the other and both have to cooperate with each other in order for the government to work.

The United Kingdom

In the British parliamentary system, the executive is collective, not singular, and is called the Cabinet. It is usually made up of 20 to 21 members, the ministers of government, headed by a prime minister. The Cabinet has the responsibility for the overall administration of national affairs, to initiate policies and coordinate the system of government.

The British Cabinet is chosen from among the members of Parliament, mainly from the elected House of Commons, with a few members from the House of Lords. The prime minister in Britain is that person who after an election is best able to command the support of the majority of members of the House of Commons. Usually that person is the leader of the party that has won the majority of seats in the House of Commons.

The prime minister appoints the Cabinet, which is usually made up of the senior members of the majority party. Note that the prime minister in Britain and in other countries with a parliamentary system is able to choose the members of the Cabinet and does not need to seek approval.

In the United States, in contrast, every single member of the Cabinet nominated by the president has to be approved by the Senate. The president nominates someone to be in the Cabinet and the Senate then has a hearing in which its members ask questions of the nominee. If the Senate at the end of the hearing does not by majority vote confirm this nominee he or she cannot become a member of the president's Cabinet.

The power of the British prime minister to hire ministers is complemented by the power to fire them. Prime Minister Tony Blair appointed 22 ministers after he became prime minister in 1997. By October 1999, 9 of the 22 were no longer in the Cabinet; some had been dismissed and some resigned. Margaret Thatcher held office from 1979 to 1990. She was elected for the second time in June 1983 and by April 1986 one-third of those who had been ministers in her first Cabinet were no longer ministers. The prime minister can also "reshuffle" the Cabinet, by reassigning ministerial responsibilities.

The prime minister's power is regarded as practically unlimited in the structure not just because he or she controls the Cabinet but also because, as head of the majority party, he or she has tremendous power over the legislature. The agenda of Parliament in Britain, in terms of what items are to be considered and debated, is determined predominantly by the prime minister.

The relationship between the executive (the Cabinet) and the House of Commons is structured on the basis of two principles:

1. The principle of collective responsibility. Each member of the Cabinet is obliged to support publicly any policies that the Cabinet has agreed on, even though he or she may disagree or may have argued against the decision within the Cabinet. If a member of the Cabinet is not willing to support a decision, the principle of collective responsibility means that person is expected to leave the government, either by resigning or being fired if the matter is particularly important. For example, between 1964 and 1990 in Britain, 21 ministers left governmental positions in the application of this principle.

2. The principle of individual responsibility. Each minister is both answerable for his own conduct and accountable for the conduct of officials falling within his or her portfolio. The application of this principle has resulted in many resignations, primarily because of personal misconduct. When a minister creates a public scandal or issues are raised in the House of Commons for which there are no acceptable explanations, resignation follows. For example, in December 1998, a minister closest to Prime Minister Blair (personal as well as political relationship), Peter Mandelson, secretary of trade and industry,

was forced to resign because he failed to disclose the fact that he had received a significant personal loan from a fellow minister who was being investigated for financial impropriety.

In contrast to the US presidential system, the British prime minister and the Cabinet can be removed from office during the five-year term if they lose the support of the majority in the House of Commons on an important issue. This can take place in one of two ways.

1. The prime minister can be removed from office and a new person voted in by a majority in the House of Commons. The new prime minister must be another member of the House of Commons, and from the same party as the departing prime minister. For example, in November 1990 the Conservative majority in that House concluded that Prime Minister Thatcher was no longer an asset. She had become more and more unpopular as she tried to force through measures with which significant sections of the British public disagreed. Hence, the majority of the Conservative Party elected a new leader, John Major, and removed Prime Minister Thatcher. This process ensures that the government does not fall. In the example the Conservative Party remained in power until 1992. Prime Minister Thatcher did not have a real option to call a general election, as the parliamentary majority wanted a change of leader, not a change of government. In most parliamentary systems in the Caribbean, in contrast, the prime minister has the option to call an election if the majority in his or her party wants a change in the person who is prime minister.

2. The government can be removed by a vote of no confidence. A vote of no confidence is one in which the majority of the House of Commons supports a resolution that it has no confidence in the government. Once a resolution of no confidence is supported by the majority of members of Parliament, the government as a whole has to resign and an election is held. This has happened, though very, very rarely. Since 1945 in Britain, the government has been removed by a vote of no confidence on only one occasion. In other parliamentary systems, governments have been removed more frequently by votes of no confidence. For example, in India, the largest democracy, since 1996 three governments and cabinets have had to resign based on votes of no confidence in the government of the day.

Hence, it could be argued that, in this regard, the parliamentary system is more flexible than the presidential system, because once a president has been elected, there is no constitutional means, except in the unusual circumstances of impeachment and conviction, for removing that president. In the parliamentary system, in theory and sometimes in practice there is some flexibility, in that the government can be forced to resign if it loses the support of a majority of the members of the legislature.

THE JUDICIARY

In both the United States and the United Kingdom, there is a hierarchical system of courts, with lower- and middle-level courts and a Supreme Court at the top of the judicial pyramid. In this discussion we are concerned with the highest court in each of these two countries.

The United States

Article 3 of the US Constitution states that there is one Supreme Court of the United States. It further determines that the Supreme Court is to be constituted by a chief justice and eight associate justices. In other words, the Supreme Court of the United States is made up of nine judges who stand at the apex of the judicial branch of state power in that presidential system.

It is interesting to consider how these judges are selected, because again we see in the selection process the American determination to have checks and balances among the different institutions of the state. Supreme Court judges are first nominated by the president. The nominees then appear before the Senate for questioning about their credentials and qualifications for the job. That process is called "confirmation hearings". It is only after these confirmation hearings, which are usually televised or broadcast on the radio, that the Senate votes for or against the president's nominee. If the Senate votes in favour of the nominee, he or she is confirmed as a judge of the Supreme Court. If the Senate votes against the nominee, he or she is rejected as a judge of the Supreme Court. This process of confirmation has on significant occasions resulted in the president's nominee being rejected by a majority of the Senate. Therefore, we see again this dimension of American government to balance one institution against the other, not to give too much power to any one branch.

Once a Supreme Court judge is confirmed he or she holds office for life. It should be noted, however, that Supreme Court judges can be removed if they are impeached and convicted in much the same way the president can be removed.

The Supreme Court of the United States is regarded as one of the most powerful of its kind among the democratic systems in the world, because it has a particular power that it uses, called "the power of judicial review". The Supreme Court has the authority to examine any law passed by Congress and approved by the president to determine whether it is constitutional or not. This authority to review legislation – either federal legislation or legislation at the state level – is an authority that the Supreme Court has used from time to time. For example, in 1954 a case was brought by the National Association for the Advancement of Colored People (NAACP) asking the court to rule on whether certain laws in some states of the United States were unconstitutional and should be struck down. The laws under review were those in the Southern states (for example, Mississippi) that made segregation in education legal; that is, blacks would attend black schools and whites would attend white schools. The Courts ruled that segregation in education was unconstitutional and should end immediately.

This ruling was of particular interest because at the time segregation was clearly supported by the majority in the Southern states. That judgement was only enforced in the Southern states by the use of military force. This case illustrates the power of the Supreme Court judgements and, even when a majority may not support the judgement, to have it enforced.

Perhaps as controversial is the recent action of the Supreme Court in December 2000 in relation to the presidential election. Voting had taken place on November 7 but in December the outcome had not yet been determined, because the votes in Florida were contested and recounts ordered in some districts. The recounts had been approved by the Florida Supreme Court but the George W. Bush campaign organization appealed to the US Supreme Court, giving reasons why the recount in Florida should be stopped. The Supreme Court, by a majority of five to four, voted to stop the recount, thereby overruling the Florida Supreme Court and ultimately ensuring that George W. Bush received the Florida electoral college votes, allowing him thereby to be confirmed as president. The following points of controversy remain:

1. Did the Supreme Court ruling violate the separation of powers – that of the separation of the judiciary from the executive? Did the judicial branch have the right to interfere in the counting of votes to determine who should be the executive elected by the people?
2. Did the Supreme Court violate the rights of the states by interfering in what could be regarded as properly a decision to be determined by the Florida Supreme Court?

As a result of these controversial issues there were significant protests in Washington and around the United States on the inauguration of George W. Bush by those who felt that this was an abuse of power. A full-page advertisement was taken out by 585 law professors stating that the Supreme Court acted improperly in its decision to stop the vote count in Florida. Nevertheless, George W. Bush was inaugurated. This case demonstrates the power of the Supreme Court in the United States.

The United Kingdom

The highest court in the United Kingdom is not an independent institution. It is part of the House of Lords (the upper house of the legislature). This judicial function is exercised by 18 or 19 judges appointed to the House of Lords by the prime minister to be the final court of appeal. The judges are called the "law lords", and they make the final determination on any judicial decision in the United Kingdom.

Unlike in the United States, Supreme Court appointments are not subject to confirmation. By convention, the prime minister appoints judges on the basis of their professionalism and not on the basis of their political partisanship. The "law lords", similar to the US Supreme Court justices, serve for life.

Up until October 2, 2000, the British "law lords" had no authority to question or to overrule any act of the British Parliament that had been properly debated and passed. In other words, they did not have the power of judicial review that the US Supreme Court can and does exercise from time to time. The reason for this is the doctrine, in the British Constitution, of "Parliamentary Sovereignty", which simply means that Parliament has supreme authority. In the United States, the Constitution is supreme. In the United Kingdom, Parliament is supreme and therefore no authority has the power to overrule acts of Parliament, once they are legitimately passed.

However, one of the more important reforms of the Blair government elected in 1997 changed that situation. In October 2000, the Human Rights Act set out in statute the rights and freedoms to which the British people are entitled. This law gives the courts the power to declare an act of Parliament either in compliance or out of compliance with the Human Rights Act.

The judicial branches of the US presidential system and the British parliamentary system have considerable differences even though they have some points in common.

11

THE ISSUE OF REFORMS

Up until the 1990s, demands for reforms in the US presidential and British parliamentary systems were more on the margin than in the mainstream. As the 1990s progressed, however, the demand for change became more widespread.

THE REFORM PROCESS IN THE UNITED STATES

The main demand for reform in the United States and the main source of dissatisfaction of the public concerns the extraordinary influence of special interests over the government. In particular, public opinion has become very vocal that the few who have great wealth, the billionaires and big corporations, have too much influence over the administration and that the main means of influencing the president and Congress is by way of financial contributions to election campaigns. For example, in 1997 a Gallup poll found that 70 percent of the American people felt that the system of campaign finance contributions needed a complete overhaul or major changes.

The reason for this dissatisfaction is not hard to find. For example, in the 2000 elections US$4 billion was spent on election campaigns by candidates for the House of Representatives, the Senate, and the presidency. The average US Senate campaign costs US$7.2 million per candidate. This money does in fact produce results. In the 1996 elections nine of every ten candidates who won their seats in the House of Representative spent more than the opposing candidate and eight of every ten senators who won their seat spent more than their opponent did.

The vast majority of the monies raised came from a small minority, from very big corporations or from very wealthy individuals. These contributors expect that one favour begets another and therefore the majority of the American people believe that this system whereby a few can give so much to the election process is a system that undermines the influence of the majority in favour of the minority.

Most of the laws regulating money in politics were passed in the 1970s because this was a period of great discontent in the United States. The dissatisfaction had to do with two events: the war in Vietnam and the Watergate scandal.

Tens of thousands of US troops were sent to fight the war in Vietnam and, ultimately, to the great disquiet of the American people, the American war machinery was defeated by these poor South-East Asian people, the Vietnamese. The United States lost over 50,000 troops and had to literally withdraw from Vietnam in the early 1970s. There were huge demonstrations against the war, because many Americans felt it was not a justifiable war. The intensity of the opposition grew when people saw on television the body bags with American soldiers and troops coming back to the United States.

The second event was the discovery that President Nixon had violated US law and this caused great discontent. The person sworn to uphold the law under the Constitution was found to have breached it and engaged in forms of corruption. This led to a great demand for reform. One of the areas that were reformed at the time was regulations dealing with the funding of elections and financing of political leaders and political organizations. Of note are three regulations that were passed in the 1970s:

1. Requirements for there to be greater transparency in reporting financial contributions to politics. Since the 1970s, each party and each candidate is required to report all donations of over US$200. The names and the identities of political donors and their financial support are publicly known. Information regarding these donations can be viewed on the Internet.
2. Limits were placed on donations to individual candidates. An upper limit of US$2,000 was placed on how much an individual can give to any one candidate; and an upper limit of US$5,000 on how much a group (political action committee) can give to an individual candidate. Political action committees are simply groups of persons in a corporation or a trade union who come together for political action. Corporations are not allowed to give money as corporations but political action committees within the corporation or trade union can make campaign contributions.
3. The requirement that there be some public funding for qualified presidential candidates. Presidential candidates who run for the major political parties – the Republican and Democratic Parties – receive a certain amount of public funding. In 1996 each candidate received US$62 million to spend on his presidential campaign. In 2000 that figure went up to US$67 million. The idea behind public funding is to reduce the dependence on private contributions.

Nevertheless, despite these rules, the influence of "big money" on politics is regarded as unacceptable. One weakness in the existing regulation is often cited as a reason for the inadequacy of the existing regulation. That is a loophole relating to what is called "soft money". Soft money refers to donations to political parties for the purpose of carrying out functions such as public education and registration of voters. There is no limit to how much the party may receive this way. Through this loophole big corporations and powerful interest groups continue to be able to exercise undue influence on how politicians behave after elections.

Perhaps the most relevant example from a Caribbean perspective is the case of the Chiquita Banana Corporation, which donated significant sums of money not to one party but to both parties in the United States during the 1990s.[1] Therefore, one of the reasons why the United States government has taken a very hostile position to banana producers in the Caribbean (St Vincent, Dominica, and Jamaica) is likely to have been that Chiquita demanded that the government should take a strong position against market competition from the Caribbean in Europe.

Another example of this undue influence is the National Rifle Association (NRA). This association commands considerable financial resources and has been able, by using financial contributions to members of Congress and to members of the administration, to block any significant gun control legislation in the United States, although opinion polls show that the majority of the American people are in favour of tighter restrictions on the sale and ownership of guns than exist at the present time. This is of great interest to us, not least of all because of the ease with which one can acquire the most sophisticated weapons in the United States and send them into Caribbean countries, in barrels, for example.

Finally, public discontent with the role of money in politics in the United States was aggravated by the exposure that in 1996 and the years following foreign money was donated to US political parties in order to influence their policies and conduct. It was revealed that money from Indonesian interests was going to the Democratic Party, at the same time that money from Hong Kong was going to the Republican Party.

As a result a number of reform proposals are now being debated to try to clean up what is an unpleasant political situation. Two of these are:

1. To place a definite upper limit on how much money wealthy candidates may spend in their own campaign.
2. To place a total ban on "soft money" donations to political parties and instead allow a certain amount of free advertising on television.

In March 2002, the Congress passed new legislation and President Bush signed into law new and more stringent campaign finance rules, albeit with continuing loopholes.

THE REFORM PROCESS IN THE UNITED KINGDOM

By the middle of the 1990s, a huge majority of the British people was of the view that their system of government needed a great deal of improvement. In 1995, 75 percent of British people believed that the structure of government needed to be significantly reformed, while only 22 percent felt that their system worked well. The main concern was that the British structure of government was based on institutions that were relics of the past and needed to be more modern, more democratic and less aristocratic.

It was hardly surprising, therefore, with public opinion strongly in favour of reforms, that the government elected in 1997 and headed by Prime Minister Tony Blair undertook a number of changes which, when taken together, are particularly significant compared to what went before and significant in relation to what still needs to be done. Seven of the major reforms carried out or in preparation since 1997 in relation to the structure and functioning of the British parliamentary system are listed below.

1. There was significant change in the composition of the House of Lords. Persons who held their positions on the basis of heredity had dominated the House of Lords for hundreds of years. In 1999, that situation was changed significantly when all but 92 of the 760 hereditary members were removed from membership in the House of Lords.

2. In September 1997, the Blair administration held a referendum, on the question of whether more power and more authority should be delegated to Scotland, Wales, and Northern Ireland. The result of the referendum was a "yes" vote and therefore national assemblies or regional parliaments were set up with some authority over these regions. Note that giving more authority to these regions did not make the United Kingdom a federation because in a unitary state the authority at the regional level is delegated from the centre rather than independent of the centre. In a federation the regional authorities have their own independent source of power based on the constitution of the federal state. In these regions of Britain the electoral system was modified to move away from the "first past the post" system, which we saw earlier was unfair to minority parties, to a form of proportional representation that allows minority parties a better chance to be represented in the legislature.

3. There was a proposal to change the electoral system from a "first past the post" system to a form of proportional representation for election to the House of Commons.

4. A referendum in May 1998 asked the people of London whether they wished to have an elected mayor to lead London as a major city. In the referendum, the people voted "yes", and significant change followed, in that after May 2000 London had an elected mayor chosen by adult suffrage among the majority of the people who live there.

5. In October 2000 the Human Rights Act was passed. This act codified the rights of the British people in one law and gave them the right to appeal to the British courts if they believed that the government was violating their rights in any significant way. Under this Human Rights Act, for the first time in British history the courts have the authority to declare that an act of the British Parliament is in violation of the provisions of the Human Rights Act. If a court found that an action by the government was not in conformity with the Human Rights Act of 2000 then the government would have to change that law to make it compliant with the Human Rights Act.

6. The Blair government in 2000 passed a law that strengthens regulation of political parties and their finances. Donations above a certain amount now need to be disclosed and anonymous donations to parties are prohibited. The reason for disclosure is that voters will know who gave, and how much, to which party and therefore may likely have undue influences.

7. Freedom of information legislation was also passed to increase public access to a wide range of government documents and information, which before 2000 would have been regarded as secret under the Official Secrets Act. Freedom of information legislation made government more open, increased the possibility of detecting acts of corruption, and strengthened the accountability of government to the people.

NOTE

1. See "The Role of Chiquita in American Politics by Way of Financial Contributions", *Time*, February 7, 2000, online edition.

THE TRANSITION FROM COMMUNISM AND POST-COMMUNISM

12

HISTORICAL OVERVIEW

The collapse of the communist system occurred between 1989 and 1991. In 1989, the Berlin Wall dividing communist East Berlin from West Berlin was torn down by the people, signalling the beginning of the end of communism in East Berlin and East Germany. Between the collapse of the Berlin Wall in 1989 and 1991 the system of communism showed further signs of strain. This reached a climax in 1991 when the most powerful of the communist states, the Soviet Union (Union of Soviet Socialist Republics, USSR), was dismantled.

This event and the process leading up to it is very distant from us in the Caribbean but, nevertheless, the collapse of communism had an impact all over the world, as post-communist societies and governments were being established. One of the effects with direct impact on the Caribbean was a substantial diversion of United States aid from other parts of the world, including the Caribbean, to the post-communist countries. This redeployment of aid was to ensure that the systems that replaced communism would be more popular and would have more support among the people in those countries than communism did.

The second major impact of the break-up of the Soviet Union is that there remained one superpower – the United States. Having two world superpowers in the United States and the Soviet Union had prevented either of them from having a free hand in global affairs because either was strong enough to check the other.

In order to look at how communism fell and what has followed we need to briefly trace the development of the system of communism. That system had its origin in the Russian Revolution, which occurred in 1917. The communist system, therefore, survived for less than 80 years. In 1917, the Russian Revolution and the system it gave rise to spread to a number of other countries, first in eastern Europe between 1944 and 1949 (for example, Yugoslavia). Then in 1949, a revolution in China led to the development of a communist system there. Cuba followed in 1959; then East Asia in the 1970s (Vietnam in particular).

By the middle of the 1980s communism existed not just in one country but in a number of states that were in alliance with each other. The communist system in the decades up to the end of the 1980s was seen as a main alternative to capitalism.

Between the 1940s and 1980s, there was a cold war between the United States and the USSR. This meant that there was very sharp competition between global capitalism, led by the United States, and international communism, led by the Soviet Union. That competition ended in 1991 when the communist system collapsed. Therefore, when we speak of the post-communist order we need to recognize that it was only ten years old in December 2001. Ten years is a short time in the life of any country and in the life of any system. Further, although the communist system has collapsed, individual communist states do remain, for example China and Cuba.

FEATURES OF COMMUNISM

We need to identify the features of the communist structure of government and of the communist state and economy. There are four significant defining features:

1. The constitution of a communist state provides that the state should be ruled by a single communist party. In effect, the fundamental law requires that the various branches of the state be dominated by the communist party. The legislative, executive, and judicial branches are all subordinated to the party. In the past, this meant that political rights and civil liberties were severely restricted. For example, in a communist state one did not have the right to form a political party and campaign in elections to transform or to change the communist system. One did not have freedom of speech to criticize the communist system; therefore, freedoms in general were also severely limited. These constitutional provisions were enforced by the power of the military and the police and therefore provided for a dictatorship.
2. The economy is predominantly state-owned and controlled. The government, through its various agencies, controls prices and owns the main factories and public utilities, the most important means of production, and the major banks and financial institutions. The communist economy is therefore referred to as a command economy, because the economy responds to the commands or directives of the state and not to the movement of the market. The free market if it exists is very limited and almost insignificant.

3. Interest groups and civic organizations (trade unions, youth organizations, and student associations) are all under the direction of the communist party.
4. Each of these states subscribe to an "official" ideology. Of course, capitalist states in general subscribe to an unofficial ideology prescribing the dominance of the private sector and the capitalist economic system and upholding liberal democracy. Jamaica, the United States, and Britain do not have official ideologies. The US Constitution does not specify that the official ideology of the United States is capitalism, whereas it was specified in the constitutions of communist states that there was an official ideology. That official ideology was *Marxism*, which took its name from the anti-capitalist German philosopher, Karl Marx. Therefore, all of the communist states have some version of Marxism inscribed in the constitution as the official ideology of the state. Individuals who did not subscribe to that ideology would find that they were discriminated against. They did not have as much opportunity and ability to advance in that society as those who were upholders of the official ideology of the state and members of the Communist Party.

These characteristics defined the communist state and made it different from other kinds of dictatorships and from democracies. Communism where it survives, like capitalism, will undergo changes. China, for example, has been the fastest growing economy in the world, with the largest amount of foreign investment. Communism in China has changed to the point where it has an increasingly important private sector, quite different from the communist system that predominated between 1917 and 1991. In Cuba the state remains dominant, but in 2001 there are private capital investments from Jamaican, Mexican, and European investors.

Communism as we have defined it here does exhibit variations, both during the time when it existed in eastern Europe and today when it continues to exist in individual countries. What makes a system essentially communist is that the communist party is constitutionally designated as the ruling party.

ASPECTS OF THE POLITICAL CULTURE

The political culture is a mixture of values and attitudes that predated communism and those that the communist regime tried to introduce. In that mixture, there are at least four aspects:

1. Dependence on government and state as provider. This dependence predated communism, because before that the Russian people looked to the tsar and the mediaeval authorities to provide for them. After the communist revolution, that tendency to depend was reinforced by aspects of communist political ideology. Paternalism – viewing the state as having an obligation to provide – was deeply embedded in the way of thinking by pre-communist as well as communist influences.

2. Prior to communism in most of the communist states, the people had a deep attachment to religion and to their particular ethnic group, defined on the basis of common language, history, and culture. The communist regime tried to undermine this. As a result there was conflict in the political culture. These pre-communist attachments were very powerful. They not only survived communism but, particularly in relation to ethnic group identities, are creating big problems for post-communism as ethnic groups fight each other based on historical antagonisms and solidarities.

3. There is great value placed on equality. The communist ideology preached that private property and capitalism led to great inequality. It socialized the people into the belief that equality would come as a consequence of getting rid of capitalism. This is one of the more successful of the endeavours of the communist system.

4. The communist system succeeded in large measure in persuading the people that social and economic rights were more important than political rights. Social and economic rights meant the right to education, housing, health care, and employment. The people were socialized into the belief that those rights were more important than the right to vote for competitive political parties or the right to form independent trade unions.

PERFORMANCE OF THE COMMUNIST SYSTEM

During the communist era, the performance of the communist system was cast in an almost totally negative light in the Western countries. Communism was portrayed in the Western media as having achieved only oppression, whereas capitalism brought only property, wealth, and advancement for the people. With the decline of communism, it is now possible to have a more objective assessment.

For example, the World Bank *Development Report* of 1996, "From Plan to Market", gives a relatively balanced evaluation of the communist system. In summary, the communist system achieved relatively strong educational advancement. Education was free at all levels and this allowed the communist states, in particular the Soviet Union, to move very quickly from backwardness and underdevelopment to become major industrial powers. Basic levels of housing and health care were also provided. Therefore, the assessment is that the social welfare performance of the communist system, starting from a relatively low base, attained considerable advances in a comparatively short time.

In terms of the economy, communist states generally maintained low inflation rates. For example, in 1990 the last year of communism in the former Soviet Union, the rate of price increase was 5 percent, and there was no unemployment. Inflation was low because the government was controlling prices by way of subsidies, and unemployment was low because people were kept working even when many were not contributing any real value. Because of the ideology of the system too often the people pretended to work and the system pretended to pay them. Relatively high levels of economic growth up to the early 1970s meant that economic growth in the Soviet Union compared very favourably to Western capitalist economic growth. In addition, there was relatively equal distribution of income.

These welfare and economic achievements were, of course, accomplished by dictatorship, lack of political freedom, restriction of civil liberties, and, sometimes, massive respression.

13

REASONS FOR THE COLLAPSE OF COMMUNISM

We can identify two very important sets of reasons for the collapse of communism: economic and political.

ECONOMIC REASONS

Economically, by the early 1980s, the performance of the communist system had begun to deteriorate in terms of economic growth and technological innovation. In particular, the communist system trailed behind the West in terms of the application of computer and information technologies to production. Computer technologies and electronics became more important as the 1980s progressed into the 1990s. Communism, therefore, in relative terms, fell behind the Western economies in levels of productivity and in terms of the quality of consumer goods. Consumer durables (televisions, washing machines, and the other articles of modern Western consumer life) were exceptionally inferior in the communist states compared to the West. For example, the motor vehicle produced in the former Soviet Union, the Lada, measures poorly in comparison to vehicles produced by Mazda and Chrysler.

This relative decline in economic performance led to deterioration in the quality of life, compared to that in the Western countries and, even more so, compared to the image that was projected of life in the United States, the United Kingdom, and other capitalist countries. These economic circumstances began to contribute to dissatisfaction, especially among the younger generation, who were more educated, more aware, and inclined to be more dissatisfied with their economic circumstances.

POLITICAL REASONS

Three political factors contributed to the collapse of communism:

1. The increasing demand for greater freedom among the people towards the end of the 1970s and the 1980s. Demands for greater freedom of speech, freedom of movement, and freedom of association are invariably strengthened with higher levels of education. The more educated a people become, the more aware they are, the less prepared they are to tolerate restrictions and to defer to traditional authority.
2. The great encouragement and support for these demands coming from the Western countries (the United States, the United Kingdom, and West Germany). This reinforced demands for greater freedom and to bring about an end to the communist system.
3. The development of disunity within the ranks of the communist party. Increasing internal division reflected itself in three positions, described below.

In the first place, there were those who felt that the communist system should be preserved at any price (the hard-line position). Second, a minority wanted to radically change the system, to get rid of the communist system and introduce some form of market economy and Western democracy. Third, in between the hard-line position and the radical one was a *reformist* point of view, which aimed to modify the communist system to make it more modern and less dictatorial in order to preserve it. In the internal balance within these parties, it was the third position that began to predominate towards the middle and end of the 1980s.

The reform position became dominant in the most important of the communist parties, namely, that of the Communist Party of the Soviet Union, which was led by Mikhail Gorbachev. He became leader of the Communist Party in 1985. At that time Gorbachev began to make changes in the economy to give more space to the private sector and allow more freedom to the people. Most important of all, Gorbachev insisted that military force should not be used against the people if they really wanted to change from the communist system. Therefore, toward the end of the 1980s, encouraged by these reforms, not pacified by them, the people began to demand less dictatorship and more democracy. Throughout the communist world there was much unconventional political behaviour, in the form of protests, roadblocks, strikes, and demonstrations, demanding more economic and political freedom. In the face of these demands and protests and Soviet leadership's position not to repress the people by military force, as had been done in the past, the communist system collapsed, and without significant bloodshed. It was predominantly a peaceful, bloodless revolution, because the reform group led by Gorbachev decided not to use the soldiers and police to shoot down the people in order to preserve the old form of communism.

By way of contrast, in 1989, the leadership of the Chinese Communist Party took a different position in response to protest. The army was used to suppress these protests, and after that bloody suppression communism survives in China. In the rest of the communist world communism was removed and post-communism was put in its place.

14

STRUCTURE OF GOVERNMENT UNDER POST-COMMUNISM

In all cases, the post-communist states established democratic governmental structures to replace the communist dictatorship. They had written constitutions that codified executives, legislatures, and judiciaries with specific characteristics.

THE EXECUTIVE

The executive in most of the post-communist states reflects a semipresidential system, perhaps most similar in the Western world to France. This means that the executive has a dual character, with a president elected directly by the people, and a prime minister appointed by the president. (For example, the Russian president, Vladimir Putin, was elected directly by the Russian people in adult suffrage elections.) The president in the semipresidential system does not sit in the legislature but the prime minister, whose appointment must be ratified by a majority of the legislature, has a seat in the legislature. This system creates a certain amount of tension between the president and the prime minister, especially if they do not share the same political party or the same political ideas.

THE LEGISLATURE

In all of these countries, after the collapse of communism, the legislature was elected for the first time from among competing political parties. The people had the right to organize parties and they used that right to organize, in most cases, a large number of political parties. As a result, in most post-communist countries there are multi-party systems. For example, in Poland in 1991, in the first post-communist free democratic election, 29 political parties won enough votes to be represented in Parliament. In Russia, in the first post-communist election, 6 political parties got over 7 percent of the votes. The number of parties represented in these legislatures showed that the people not only had freedom of association but they were using that freedom to make their politics more democratic and more competitive.

The electoral system used in these elections did not copy the systems in the United States or the United Kingdom. The "first past the post" system used in these countries discriminates in favour of the majority parties and against third parties and smaller parties of one kind or another. In the post-communist democracies, the "first past the post" system was combined with proportional representation, thus instituting a fairer and more balanced electoral system, as exists, for example, in Germany.

THE JUDICIARY

In these countries, great effort was made to ensure that the judicial branch was independent because under communism this branch had been dominated by politics. Therefore, there was concern that, in the new democracy, this branch would not be dominated by any political party but would be independent and strong. One way of doing this was by providing in each constitution for the judiciary to have the power of judicial review. The power of judicial review gave the judicial branches in post-communist states the constitutional authority to overrule laws passed by the legislature and approved by the executive, if it determines that those laws are in breach of the constitution.

RESULTS OF ELECTIONS FOLLOWING COMMUNISM

The results of the first elections were the same in almost every post-communist democracy. The communist parties and leaders were voted out of office and out of government. In most cases, they received a very small percentage of the vote, and therefore lost power. There were two exceptions to this general rule, in Bulgaria and Romania.

By the late 1990s, however, communist candidates and reformed communist parties had begun to gather popular support. In the Russian elections of December 1993, the Communist Party won 12 percent of the votes. This had grown to 22 percent by the elections of December 1995. In June 1996, the presidential election was held in Russia, with many different candidates. The two most popular candidates were the former president Boris Yeltsin, the anti-communist/democratic candidate, and Zyuganov, the communist candidate. In the first round of the election, Yeltsin won 35 percent of the votes and Zyuganov 32 percent of the votes. In keeping with the Russian Constitution, a second round of voting was held, because none of the candidates had an absolute majority. In this round the third-place candidate dropped out and Yeltsin won 54 percent of the votes and Zyuganov 40 percent. In the last presidential election, held in June 2000, Yeltsin's successor, Vladimir Putin won with a significant 53 percent, beating the communist candidate, who got 30 percent of the votes.

It is apparent that, in terms of voting behaviour and electoral support under the post-communist democratic system, a significant number of people in post-communist countries support communist candidates. In several of these countries, communists have been voted back into power. The difference is that in the post-communist system, the communists can be voted out of power because it is a democratic system. Under communism there was no such possibility, because the constitution declared that the communist party was the state power.

According to surveys published in the *Journal of Democracy*, January 2001, in 16 post-communist countries in Europe, only 47 percent of citizens positively endorsed their new system of government. In Russia 29 percent of the people wanted a return to communist rule.

15

THE POST-COMMUNIST ECONOMY

The post-communist economy is characterized by the dismantling of the state-dominated command economy. Post-communist states moved from being command economies to become market economies, in which a major feature was a reduction of the role of the state. This meant that the state would no longer own the means of production and would now have a primarily regulatory role, with the free market the driving force in the economic system.

In practical terms, this meant that subsidies from the state would be significantly reduced, if not eliminated. Subsidies that kept prices down were removed substantially, if not totally, and subsidies that kept inefficient or unproductive enterprises open and provided unproductive employment were significantly removed or eliminated.

The move from command economy to free market also meant that the state cut back on its expenditure in education, health, and generally in the provision of welfare. Part of the reason for these cuts in social service was that the state now had far fewer resources, because it no longer owned enterprises that generated a certain level of profits. The first general reality of the post-communist economy was a state that was doing far less and a market that was doing far more.

At the same time, as this command economy was being dismantled, new investments were coming in, mainly from the Western capitalist countries, including the United States. US authorities had an obvious interest in ensuring that the people would favour the new system over the old communist regime. These new investments, while they were significant, were inadequate to deal with the massive task of reconstruction and modernization of these new economies.

The immediate consequences and the continuing results of these changes were quite dramatic in a number of areas:

1. *Cost of living*. In Russia, which is the most important post-communist country, inflation in the last year of communism was 5 percent. By 1992, after the first full year of a post-communist economy, the inflation rate had moved to 1,354 percent. In 1993

inflation began to decline, but was still 883 percent. By 1995 the rate of inflation was 197 percent.

2. *Growth in unemployment.* Unemployment grew because many, who previously had been in jobs that were artificially created, lost employment. These jobs were not really adding value but under communism people nevertheless had some work and some income. In the market economy, enterprises survived only on the basis of being competitive and efficient.

3. *Economic decline.* Economic growth did not occur but, instead, there was economic decline, because fewer enterprises were producing and new enterprises were being opened at a rate that was inadequate to fill the gap left by those being closed. There-fore, in terms of economic growth performance, during the period 1990 to 1998, the annual growth rate of the Russian economy was –7.1 percent. This meant that the GDP of Russia, both per capita and overall, was less than in 1990. This economic indicator had an impact on social indicators, because economic performance is the foundation for the social indices of any coun-try. Life expectancy, for example, at the close of the 1990s was lower than in the last years of communist rule. In respect of law and order, violent crimes grew. Corruption increased as many of the previous communist supporters sought to use their posi-tions in order to hold wealth and to acquire wealth in corrupt ways.

4. *Greater inequality.* In a command economy, the state tried with some success to keep the gaps between the social strata from growing too wide (even though many officials at the top were looking after themselves). With the market economy inequali-ties began to increase significantly.

In the political arena, post-communism presented substantial positive changes to the people in these countries. In the economic and social arenas the picture is at best a mixed one and at worse that of a harder life, with higher prices, higher levels of unemployment, and more crime than under the previous system.

Against this background, various opinion surveys have been carried out. In 1992 to 1993, surveys done by the US Agency for International Development across ten post communist states revealed that in nine of the ten, the majority of the people felt that their economic situation was worse. In nine of the ten, the people felt that the post-communist system was better than the previous one, and in eight of ten the majority felt that the free market economy was better for their country, even though they said that the situation was worse.

Perhaps the most important finding of these surveys is that, in nine of the ten states the majority gave an economic rather than a political definition of democracy. By economic definition, they meant that they expected democracy ultimately to improve economic justice, improve their standard of living, and create improving levels of equality. As far as they were concerned democracy should mean more social justice, a better quality of life, and less inequality. In their definition these are more important than the political definition of democracy, with its emphasis on political rights.

We can understand this definition if we recall their political culture. They have a long history of expecting things to be done for them economically and socially. Part of the reason for overthrowing the communist state was that it was failing economically. The economic priorities are deeply ingrained in their way of thinking and their way of life. As the post-communist system develops, if there is no economic improvement, this has implications for how far the people will continue to support post-communism, because of their economic understanding of what democracy ought to be.

This is quite different from many other countries, for example, in the Caribbean, where the general and popular understanding of democracy is more political than economic. Freedom, to speak, to vote or not to vote, to protest, is of primary importance.

PROSPECTS OF POST-COMMUNIST SYSTEMS

It is likely that the post-communist economies will stabilize from the extraordinary instability of the first years and that this will provide the basis for some growth. However, this is not likely unless the state plays a bigger role in the market economy.

The democratic system is likely to be sustained, but democracy in the post-communist countries is likely to be somewhat different from the democratic system in the Western world, because the political culture of the people is different. It is also likely to be different because, unlike in the Western countries, the communist and socialist parties are likely to have strong popular support.

Social unrest is likely to continue because of low levels of social cohesion based on ethnic differences, high levels of crime, and the absence of strong systems of public order.

Surveys conducted in post-communist Russia between 2000 and 2001 indicate public opinion trends more or less in line with these prospects. For example, 73 percent of a nationwide survey in February 2001 felt that market reforms should either be ceased or continued under strict state control. Price increases, rising crime, and increased unemployment cause greatest anxiety among the people, yet there are significant positive views about the future of the economic and political system.[1]

NOTE

1. See http://russiavotes.org/Mood-rus-cur.htm.

THE ANGLOPHONE CARIBBEAN STATE: DECOLONIZATION, CONTEMPORARY CONSTITUTIONS, AND REFORM PROPOSALS

16

DECOLONIZATION

Independent Caribbean states, such as Jamaica, Trinidad and Tobago, Barbados, and St Kitts and Nevis, are just about 40 years old. The post-communist states we looked at in the previous section were approaching 10 years old, and the United States and the United Kingdom are well over 200 years old. The year 2002 marks the fortieth anniversary of the first independent state, Jamaica, and therefore the Caribbean states are still relatively young.

Jamaica's independence from Britain in August 1962 meant the need for an independence constitution. The structure of the state had to be documented, in order for this new nation to develop its political life. That independence constitution came at the end of a process we call *decolonization* – the removal of colonial rule.

THE PROCESS OF DECOLONIZATION

Decolonization began in 1938 with unconventional political behaviour, social unrest, and islandwide protests against the conditions of that time. Unconventional behaviour is usually disruptive but out of that disruption very often comes positive change. For example, anticolonial war brought about the birth of the United States; protests helped bring about the change from communism to post-communist states; so, too, in the Caribbean unconventional behaviour, very often illegal, even life-threatening, started the final stages in the process of decolonization, which ended in Jamaica's independence. The behaviour of the people in Jamaica in the 1930s was not unique; in every territory in the Caribbean, with no exception, the people engaged in similar kinds of protest in the 1930s and 1940s.

The original plan for West Indian decolonization was to have the states become independent within the context of a federation. The Federation of the West Indies was formed in 1958 and was similar to federations that were being formed in other parts of the British Empire undergoing decolonization. The West Indies Federation collapsed in 1961, having lasted only three years.

The main underlying reason for the collapse was that the federation did not have sufficient grassroots support, particularly in rural Jamaica. Because it did not have popular support, disagreements that developed among the leadership precipitated the collapse of the federation. In 1961, a referendum was held in Jamaica in which the Jamaican people were asked to decide whether Jamaica should remain in the federation. The majority of the people voted to leave the federation. In the referendum of 1961, the majority of urban Jamaica (the more educated part of the country) voted to remain in the federation. The majority of the rural population voted to leave the federation. One reason for this was the view that Jamaica's progress should not be held back by what were then regarded as smaller, poorer islands. When Jamaica voted to leave the federation there were ten Caribbean countries involved. Dr Eric Williams, then head of the Trinidad and Tobago government, made his famous statement, "Ten minus one equals zero", thereby signalling Trinidad's withdrawal from, and the effective end of, the federation.

Forty years later, not only have some of these smaller islands moved ahead of Jamaica in terms of per capita income and levels of human development, but business people from these islands are coming to Jamaica in order to invest in and save Jamaican businesses from collapsing or being bought by North American and British capital. One reason for the relative strength of the Trinidadian economy, for example, has to do with patterns of consumption and investment that differ between Trinidad and Jamaica. In Port of Spain you will not see the number of Mercedes-Benz and BMW motor vehicles as you will see in Kingston, but the factories in Trinidad have state-of-the-art machinery. In comparison the factories in Jamaica have machinery that is 25 to 30 years old. Not surprisingly, then, the supermarkets in Jamaica are stocked with Trinidadian goods that are better packaged and better priced than Jamaican goods. Having collapsed the federation in 1961, we are now, in the twenty-first century, beginning to see the need for a single market and economic unit. Hence, we are now establishing the Caribbean Single Market and Economy (CSME). Had the federation not broken up in 1961, that CSME would have been a reality long ago and we would have been better prepared for the adversities as well as the opportunities of globalization.

THE INDEPENDENCE CONSTITUTION DRAFTED BY JAMAICA IN 1962

The constitution of the independent Jamaican nation established a parliamentary type of democracy patterned on the British model. It was patterned on the British model, for two reasons:

1. That was the type of government to which our leaders had grown accustomed in the decolonization process.
2. That was the type of democracy on the basis of which the British were willing to concede independence. If there had been a proposal for an American type of government, the British would likely have been doubtful. There was no real consideration at that time of a presidential type of democracy.

What may not have been appropriate then may well be considered more appropriate now. We should recognize that in the 1960s, just as deferential leadership was appropriate then but is less appropriate now, so too the parliamentary system, considered very appropriate then, is now being brought into question as to whether it is appropriate given the conditions of 2001 and beyond.

The Jamaican Constitution became the model that was followed more or less closely by the other Caribbean states, 12 of which became independent between 1962 and 1983. In those years each newly emerging Caribbean state looked at the Jamaican structure of government and the Jamaican Constitution and, to one extent or another, reproduced the Jamaican model in their particular system.

The Constitution was not put to a referendum. It was decided on by the leaders, who agreed on the British parliamentary type of democracy, which Jamaica and all the other Caribbean countries still have, with the exception of Guyana. Guyana in 1980 changed its parliamentary system to a presidential system, different, in many ways, from presidential systems in the United States and other countries in that great power is concentrated in the executive in ways that other presidential systems do not.

17

FEATURES OF CARIBBEAN
PARLIAMENTARY DEMOCRACIES

THE EXECUTIVE

The executive in the typical Caribbean state is the principal instrument of policy for the country and is also responsible for the coordination of the entire government. This executive, like the British executive, is made up of a prime minister and a Cabinet, chosen from the legislature. They must be members of the legislature and are responsible to the legislature, in keeping with the theory of the British Constitution. We can say there is a combination of powers rather than a separation of powers, in that the executive and the legislature are not separated in the way that they are in the US presidential system.

The Caribbean prime minister has all the powers of the British prime minister and takes unto himself or herself more powers. The main powers of the prime minister in the Caribbean are listed below.

1. The prime minister hires and fires ministers. For example, in 2001–2002 in Trinidad and Tobago, Prime Minister Panday dismissed two of his ministers and one resigned, creating a crisis in the government.
2. The prime minister, alone, determines the responsibility of each of the ministers. For example, in Jamaica, in September 2001 the prime minister changed around the portfolio responsibilities of his ministers, in what is called a Cabinet reshuffle.
3. The prime minister chairs Cabinet meetings and therefore has great power to determine what gets discussed and whose opinion is heard.
4. The prime minister determines the legislative agenda, which means that he or she determines what laws are proposed to be put before the legislature for debate and approval.
5. The prime minister determines when Parliament is dissolved and sets the date for new elections within the five-year period required by the Constitution.

6. The prime minister has significant powers of appointment. He or she appoints important public officials (similar to the British prime minister). For example, the prime minister determines who becomes the head of the army and also appoints a significant number of members of the upper house or Senate. For example, in Grenada almost 80 percent of the members of the Senate are appointed by the prime minister. In Trinidad and Tobago a little more than half, and in Jamaica almost two thirds, of the senators are appointed by the prime minister.

THE LEGISLATURE

The legislature in all the Caribbean states has the constitutional responsibility to make the laws of the particular country. These legislatures have two chambers, like the British, except for Dominica, St Kitts and Nevis, St Vincent and the Grenadines, and Guyana, which have only one chamber.

The elected chamber, the House of Representatives, is chosen on the basis of universal adult suffrage (all adults have the right to vote). The elections are conducted on the basis of the "first past the post" electoral system, adopted from the British system. In Caribbean elections, this system discriminates in favour of the majority parties and against third parties and minority parties. For example, in Grenada in 1999, the winning party received 62 percent of the votes, and the opposition party 38 percent. However, the system operated in such a way in Grenada that the winning party with 62 percent of the votes got 100 percent of the seat in the House of Representatives. This is an extreme example of how this system can operate. It is based not on the percentage of votes one gets but how geographically concentrated is that percentage of the vote.

Under these constitutions the legislature has the power to remove the government on a resolution of a vote of no confidence. When that vote is supported by a majority of members of the legislature the government is forced to resign. To remove the executive in that way where the governing party has a small majority in the elected house requires that some members of the governing party in the legislature vote against the government. For example, in November 2001 when Prime Minister Panday of Trinidad and Tobago lost the support of three of his members of Parliament, he faced being removed from office, because the Parliament was made up of 19 members of his political party and 17 of the opposition. To avoid this, he called a general election in December 2001, even though elections had been held in 2000 and were not required to be held again until December 2005.

THE JUDICIARY

The judiciary in the Caribbean has some powers of judicial review – to determine whether an action by the executive is in breach of the constitution.

The judiciary in the Caribbean has somewhat more power in constitutional terms than the British judiciary in this regard, because there is no written constitution in Britain, whereas there is one in each of the Caribbean states.

The highest judges within the judiciary, in the Caribbean, are appointed on the recommendation of the prime minister. The chief justice and the president of the Court of Appeal are also appointed on the recommendation of the prime minister. This is not different from Britain, where the prime minister has similar powers. This power of appointment extends to other important officials of state. Top civil servants, for example, in each of the Caribbean states are appointed by commissions and the majority of the members of these commissions are appointed by the prime ministers.

Finally, the judiciary, under the independence constitutions, has as its final court the Privy Council in the United Kingdom. The Privy Council is the highest court, so that an appeal would go through the Supreme Court, then the Court of Appeal, and finally to the Privy Council in England. Currently there is some controversy around the need for, and the method of establishing, a Caribbean Court of Justice to replace the Privy Council as the highest court.

There is an important difference between the judicial branch of government in Caribbean states and the judiciary in the British state. In the Caribbean the highest level of the judiciary (the Privy Council) is located outside of the Caribbean, whereas in Britain it is located in the House of Lords.

FUNDAMENTAL HUMAN RIGHTS AND FREEDOMS

Each Caribbean constitution, starting with that in Jamaica, provided for freedoms and rights consistent with a democracy. Freedom of speech, of conscience, and of assembly are all written into the constitutions but these rights are also qualified and subject to a number of conditions. In the Jamaican case, the Fundamental Rights section of the Constitution can be suspended by a special act of Parliament for a specified period. There has been much dissatisfaction with the fact that the constitutions seem to give rights to the people but limit them or, in some cases, even take them away under certain circumstances.

DIFFERENCES BETWEEN THE PARLIAMENTARY SYSTEM IN BRITAIN AND THE CARIBBEAN

In the Caribbean, the prime minister has greater power and dominance over the executive than in Britain. The prime ministers of Jamaica, Barbados, and Trinidad and Tobago are generally more powerful in relation to the executive or Cabinet than the prime minister of Britain in relation to that executive or Cabinet. This stems from the fact that members of the Cabinet in Britain are more likely than their Caribbean counterparts to take a stand that opposes the prime minister. In Britain, on a number of occasions, particularly under Prime Minister Margaret Thatcher, Cabinet ministers threatened to leave the Cabinet as a result of disagreement. This was a restraining influence on the prime minister, because no prime minister wishes to have senior members of his or her party leave the government in any significant number.

In the Caribbean, this is much less likely to happen, for a number of reasons. The first is economics – in Britain, the ministers of government tend to be less dependent on politics and better able to survive outside of the political arena. Caribbean ministers, on the other hand, are more dependent on their government positions, as well as on government favours, and are therefore less willing to resign or risk being fired. In the Caribbean ministers are unable or unwilling to consider survival outside of the Cabinet, because either their professions are not sufficiently established or the government controls so much of the work indirectly or directly that leaving the government may prejudice their ability to earn a substantial income or to achieve an equivalent level of living. The second reason is more cultural or psychological, and it is, as we have seen, that in the Caribbean traditionally, the political culture is one of deference to the leader, and thus government ministers are less likely to disagree with the prime minister.

The second major difference between the British and Caribbean parliamentary systems relates to the power of the prime minister over the legislature. This is greater in the Caribbean parliamentary system than in the British parliamentary system. In the British Parliamentary system, the prime minister is often opposed by members of his or her own party within the legislature. Members are often free to vote against the prime minister and against the government position. Usually, these are "backbenchers", who do not have Cabinet appointments. In the Caribbean, it would be highly unusual for a member of the legislature belonging to the prime minister's party to oppose him or her. There are a number of reasons for this:

1. In the Caribbean there are relatively few members who are not ministers, and each is just waiting to become a minister, so that instead of "back-benchers" they may be characterized as "ministers in waiting". They are not likely to oppose the person who has the power to determine whether they become ministers of government. This has to do with scale and size. In the British House of Commons there are 659 members, 22 of which are ministers and there are perhaps another 30 who are deputy ministers, which leaves hundreds who do not have any real

prospects of getting a ministerial appointment. By contrast in the Caribbean, for example in Trinidad and Tobago, there are 36 members of the House of Representatives. In the current government, 19 are members of the ruling party, and 16 of those are ministers. Therefore, the three who are not ministers have a real chance of being given a portfolio if one of their colleagues resigns or is fired. This becomes a disincentive to opposing the prime minister because it reduces the likelihood of moving up to Cabinet status.

2. Another reason is the cultural factor. In the Caribbean the prime minister exercises more control over his party than the British prime minister. This means that a member of the legislature cannot hope to stand in the next election if he or she incurs the disfavour of the prime minister, since party candidates are approved by the leader. In Britain the candidate for election is chosen by the people in the constituency.

3. Finally, Caribbean constitutions give the prime minister the power to dissolve Parliament if a majority of members would change the prime minister or vote no confidence in the government. For example, what happened to Prime Minister Margaret Thatcher in Britain in 1990, when the members of her party in the House of Commons fired her and chose someone else, could not happen in the Caribbean because the prime minister has the power to dissolve Parliament and call an election. Only three Caribbean countries do not give the prime minister this power; St Lucia, St Vincent and the Grenadines, and Belize. The power of the prime minister over the legislature is therefore stronger in the Caribbean than in Britain.

The Caribbean legislature is less powerful than the British Parliament, not just in relation to the prime minister, but also because the Caribbean legislature is subject to a codified constitution. In Britain, there is no codified constitution and therefore there are no constitutional limits on the power of the legislature. This leads to some very interesting anomalies and contradictions. For example, it is entirely possible, theoretically, that the British Parliament by a simple vote could end the monarchy. The Jamaica Parliament could not do this because under the Jamaican codified constitution, this could only happen by way of a referendum. The Constitution limits and defines the power of the legislature in a way that does not exist in the United Kingdom.

In the Caribbean the prime minister's power of appointment is constantly plagued with controversy, because of the charge that Caribbean prime ministers make appointments on the basis of political loyalty, rather than qualifications. For example, in Jamaica the appointment of the present governor general, Sir Howard Cooke, was not an appointment of consensus where the opposition and the government agreed. This appointment was supported by the governing party but attacked by the opposition as being simply an appointment of someone who is a strong supporter of the governing People's National Party. Similarly, the president of the Court of Appeal was named as Justice Rattray and again this appointment was attacked as being a partisan appointment rather than one based on professional consideration. Hence, the convention that appointments to sensitive public positions are non-partisan, or appear to be, seems to be more easily violated in the Caribbean than in the United Kingdom.

The major recurring difference between the Caribbean and British parliamentary systems is the greater power of the prime minister over the parliamentary constitutional system within the Caribbean context compared to the British.

18

CONSTITUTIONAL REFORM

Against the background of this discussion of the powers held by the branches of government in the Caribbean, we can examine the demands for constitutional reform that have been quite strong in various Caribbean states. For example, in Barbados in 1998, a Constitutional Reform Commission was appointed. This commission reported in 1999 and changes to the Barbados Constitution are now being debated. In other Caribbean territories, at different times, there have been demands for constitutional change and the appointment of commissions to make recommendations concerning how the constitutions should be changed. In Jamaica, important changes are being debated in relation to the Constitution in general and the Bill of Rights in particular.

MAIN AREAS OF AGREEMENT

There are six areas in which there is general agreement among political leaders and within civil society that these constitutions need to be changed:

1. The head of state should no longer be a representative of the British monarch but the head of state should represent the Caribbean people. In other words, there is general agreement on the need for a republican form of government.
2. The fundamental rights and freedoms laid out in the constitutions should be strengthened and better protected. It should be more difficult to restrict the rights of the people.
3. The power of the executive, and the prime minister in particular, is too great and needs to be more limited than it is now.
4. The legislature has too little independence and needs to be more independent to be better able to restrain the executive and represent the people.
5. The Privy Council should no longer be the highest court of appeal. The highest court of appeal ought to be a Caribbean court and not a British one.

6. Public officials, including parliamentarians and politicians, are insufficiently accountable to the people and therefore a way has to be found to make politicians, civil servants, and public officials generally more accountable to the people.

Alongside these areas of agreement and within some of these areas, there are big differences on how these should be reflected in constitutional change. For example, in relation to item 5 above, two big disagreements within this agreement are when to discontinue appeals to the judicial committee of the British Privy Council and whether the people should make this decision by referendum. This is such an important issue that many believe that a referendum should be held and the people and not the government should decide whether to support a Caribbean Court of Justice in place of the Privy Council.

In general, however, there are two lines of thought on how to change the constitution: by radical or moderate reform.

RADICAL PROPOSALS FOR CONSTITUTIONAL REFORM

Advocates of the radical line of thought argue the need to change the British parliamentary system to a presidential type of democracy. They argue that the British parliamentary system is no longer working, but instead is deteriorating, and therefore it should be changed. The proposals call for radical change in two areas: first, instituting a Caribbean presidential system, and second, instituting more direct mechanisms of democracy. The proposals falling under this general heading can be summarized as follows.

The Executive

1. The head of government or the effective executive (whether called prime minister or president) in the Caribbean should be directly elected as in presidential systems in the United States and elsewhere. The head of government is not thereby representing a particular constituency but is voted for by the entire electorate.
2. This directly elected head of government should not sit in the legislature. The legislature should be a separate institution with the directly elected executive having the right to appear before it but not to membership in it.
3. This directly elected head of government should not be removable by the legislature.
4. The directly elected head of government should have a fixed number of terms. Under this proposal, for example, Prime Minister Vere Bird in Antigua would not have been able to lead the government for approximately 30 years.

The Legislature

Radical reform proposes that the legislature should be elected separately from the executive. In effect, in any election the voter would have at least two legal votes: one for head of the government (the person whom the voter regards as best able to lead the country and to guide the government); and a second vote for a member of the legislature to represent his or her constituency. This second vote may be for a candidate from a different political party and not be from the same party as that of the person the voter believes is best able to run the country. This is called a split vote – one vote for the head of government and another for the constituency representative.

The legislature elected in this way would have a fixed term, so that, unlike the present situation, the head of government would not be able to dissolve the legislature. This would mean that the members of the legislature would be able to vote against a proposal from the president, without the fear that this would bring about either an end to the term of the legislature or alternatively bring down the president and end the tenure of the government.

Under these radical reform proposals, other features of the legislature are that:

1. The members of the legislature would have a legal obligation to report to their constituencies at certain specified intervals, and they would be breaking the law if they did not.
2. The constitution and the law would give the constituency the right of recall. Constituents would therefore be able to recall a member of Parliament if they were dissatisfied with his or her performance and have another election for that constituency. This proposal is advocated on the grounds that if a member of the legislature knew that the people had that power this would deter the neglect that too often takes place (where the candidate is seen at the time of the election campaign but not again for another five years).

Other Radical Reform Measures

1. The members of the Cabinet (government ministers) and those appointed to sensitive positions in the judiciary and in the public sector would be appointed by the head of the government but would be drawn from outside the legislature. Having been nominated the candidate would have to undergo a confirmation process. The people, through the legislature, would have a chance to hear the person's qualifications, know the person's experience, and then the legislature would then vote.

2. The referendum should be used more frequently as a means of public decision making. Under this proposal, the people would have the opportunity to vote on important issues. The precedent is the referendum in Jamaica in 1961. The proposal is being put forward by the 1998 Barbados Constitutional Reform Commission that at the time of an election, a certain percentage of the electorate would be able to propose that a particular question be put on the ballot (for example, whether marijuana should be legalized). This issue would not be decided by the elected representatives but would be put on the ballot. The people would vote and Parliament would have no choice but to formulate the law to put the people's decision into effect. This use of the referendum is called "The Use of Power of the Initiative" in the United States. Another application of this proposal would be to decide on the issue of whether to establish a Caribbean Court of Justice.

3. The advocates of radical reform wish the electoral system to be changed from the existing "first past the post" system to one that combines constituency representation with proportional representation in a manner that would be less discriminatory.

These points amount to a radical shift from the parliamentary system on the grounds that this system has failed and that the political culture has changed to the point where the people and the politics would benefit from something new and radical.

MODERATE PROPOSALS
FOR CONSTITUTIONAL REFORM

The radical position described above is strongly opposed by a second line of thinking, that instead of changing the British parliamentary system for another type, we need to modify and improve this system. The proposals therefore aim to address the weaknesses and not to get rid of what we have known for the last 40 or more years.

Proponents of this line propose the following:

1. The president should be a non-executive president, who would be chosen by the Parliament and not by the people. Once the Parliament is elected, the Senate and the House of Representatives would select, by a two thirds majority, the person to be president. The person would have been nominated by the prime minister after consultation with the leader of the opposition.

2. This ceremonial president would have some responsibilities beyond the existing functions of the governor general. The president would have the ultimate voice in selecting key officials, such as the chief justice and the president of the Court of Appeal.

3. The prime minister would have some restrictions on the powers that he or she now exercises. Under this proposal, the number of ministers that the prime minister could appoint would be limited by the constitution. For example, one of the suggestions in the Jamaican reform debate is that the prime minister would be limited to being able to appoint no more than 40 percent of the total number of members of Parliament. This would limit the power of the prime minister over the legislature.

4. There would be modifications to the parliamentary system to make it more effective. The main change would be to strengthen the parliamentary committees, such as those with oversight of the economy, national security, and foreign affairs. The following proposals would be implemented:

   - Each of the committees of Parliament would be chaired by a member of the opposition party. For example, the Public Accounts Committee in all of the islands is one of the more effective committees because it is chaired by a member of the opposition.
   - The committees would have a majority of government members.
   - No government minister would be allowed to be a member of a committee with related oversight. For example, the Committee on Education would be chaired by the person in the opposition having responsibility for education. The committee would have a majority of government members but it would not include the minister of education. This would make the Parliament more effective, by increasing the likelihood of the parliamentary committee exposing to the public actions or proposals by government that are not in the national interest or are weak and unjustified.

5. In this modified parliamentary system, fundamental rights and freedoms would be entrenched in such a way as to make it extremely difficult for the government or Parliament to restrict the rights of the people. To ensure this protection the Bill of Rights or, as it is being called in Jamaica, the Charter of Rights, would ordinarily be beyond the capacity of the government by itself to restrict or to limit.

6. Public officials, including ministers of government and others, such as commissioners of police, would be subject to impeachment for serious misconduct, corruption, or abuse of power. The impeachment procedure would have to be carried out by a process defined in the constitution. This process, as it is now being recommended in Jamaica, would include two stages: (1) The first is that a complaint would be brought before a joint select committee of Parliament on impeachment. The complaint

could be brought by three members of Parliament plus 1,000 signatures of citizens. The joint select committee of Parliament on impeachment would be made up of seven persons, chosen as follows: three by the prime minister, three by the leader of the opposition, and the seventh would be the president of the Senate. The duty of this committee would be to investigate the charges and determine whether there is a case. (2) If there is deemed to be a case it goes to the second stage, which is the impeachment tribunal. This tribunal is made up of five non-parliamentarians, one chosen by the prime minister, one by the leader of the opposition and three others chosen by the president after consultation with the prime minister and the leader of the opposition. The tribunal then hears the case and the guilt or innocence of the official established by majority vote. The impeachment process would be subject to judicial review.

To summarize, proponents of this line of thinking argue for retaining the parliamentary system but modifying it in ways that will make the system work better, by making the prime minister and parliamentarians more accountable and ensure that the politics is less a source of dissatisfaction.

THE MAIN CRITICISMS OF THE RADICAL AND MODERATE REFORMS PROPOSED FOR CARIBBEAN CONSTITUTIONS

Proposals for radical change are criticized, first on the general grounds that the presidential system is unfamiliar, alien to the Caribbean, its history, and its system of government, and is therefore inappropriate.

A second objection to radical reform is that the presidential system of democracy has too great a risk that the executive and the legislature may not agree and instead of resulting in good government there will be bad government or no government when the branches of government are unable to reach agreement. In the US system, this is called gridlock.

The argument against the moderate proposals is that these reforms do not change the fundamental problem in the Caribbean parliamentary democracy, which is the concentration of power in the executive and in the hands of the prime minister. It circumscribes it, but it leaves the prime minister essentially an elected dictator.

CONTEMPORARY CARIBBEAN POLITICS: GLOBALIZATION, REGIONALISM, AND POLITICAL CHANGE

19

CONTEMPORARY CARIBBEAN POLITICS

POSITIVE ASPECTS

1. Freedom is a fundamental achievement of Caribbean politics and society. An annual survey of freedom in the world is carried out by quite an established and reputable organization based in the United States, called Freedom House, which looks at the status of freedom in all the countries of the world. Freedom House looks at two dimensions of freedom: first, at political rights, such as the freedom to form political parties, the right to vote, or the extent to which there is choice and open competition in elections; and second, at civil liberties, which include religious rights, freedom of the press, and freedom of association (ability to form your own youth club or citizens association). They score each of the states around the world according to how far they recognize in practice political rights and civil liberties. On that measure the annual survey of freedom in the world places all Caribbean states in the category of "free states", with one exception – Antigua and Barbuda – which is classified as partly free. One of the reasons is the extent to which freedom of the press is restricted by the dominance of the Bird family in Antigua and Barbuda. There is a third lowest rank of "unfree", into which no anglophone Caribbean state falls.

2. In the English-speaking Caribbean governments are removed and oppositions put into office through elections that are relatively free and fair. This has been so for the last 50 years. There is no other region in the world, in Africa, Asia, Latin America, North America, or Europe, in which governments have been removed and oppositions put in office so consistently by elections as in the Caribbean. In every other region of the world, there have been coups, such as the one that took place in Pakistan in 1999. In every other region of the world, there has been one-party dictatorship, to one extent or another, or the assassination of leaders of government. In the United States, for example, in the last 35 years, one president and

an attorney general have been assassinated and there has been an attempted assassination of another president. Leaders of US civil society such as Martin Luther King and Malcolm X were also murdered. In India, the world's largest democracy, three prime ministers have been assassinated in the last 50 years.

3. Within the last 10 years, all countries of the world have been assessed in relation to their levels of human development. This rating takes into account three factors: (1) per capita income, (2) average life span of the population, and (3) education. The 2002 UNDP *Human Development Report* groups 173 states according to their levels of human development into three categories: high, medium, and low human development. The 12 English-speaking Caribbean states are evaluated and ranked in the annual report. Five of these states, Barbados, the Bahamas, Antigua and Barbuda, St Kitts and Nevis, and Trinidad and Tobago, are ranked in the highest level. The other Caribbean states are ranked in the category of medium human development. None are ranked in the category of low human development.

NEGATIVES ASPECTS

1. There has been a deterioration or decay in systems of democracy or what is sometimes called democratic governance. One area that stands out in this regard is the criminal justice system. This can be attributed to corruption in the police forces, abuse of citizens' rights by the police, delays in the court system, and deplorable prison conditions, which rank among the worst in the world. Within the executives, there are at least three countries in which ministers of government have been implicated in corruption in the last two decades of the twentieth century: Antigua and Barbuda, the Bahamas, and Jamaica, as well as in the leadership of the political parties in St Kitts and Nevis.

2. Despite good economic performance in many Caribbean states, rates of unemployment and underemployment are relatively high throughout the region. The levels of poverty are also relatively high. Crime levels are also high, especially violent crimes, increasingly related to the transshipment of illicit narcotics, in particular cocaine. This illicit traffic is presenting huge dangers not just to the criminal justice system but to the survival of democracy itself.

3. Declining electoral turnout in the Caribbean and increasing unconventional political participation across the region are features of Caribbean politics. This trend reflects growing dissatisfaction with the performance of democratic institutions,

though not with democracy as a value. Institutions in which confidence is declining include political parties, parliaments, political leaders, and prime ministers across the region.

We can therefore see both positives and negatives if we conduct an objective assessment of Caribbean politics. We can also argue that the negatives are more dynamic than the positives. Both the positive and negative aspects of contemporary Caribbean politics are partially related to the position of Caribbean states, economies, and societies in the process of globalization.

20

GLOBALIZATION

Globalization is a process. A process differs from a system in that it is dynamic whereas a system is static. Globalization is a process in which geographic, economic, and cultural boundaries are of decreasing significance, first and foremost to the movement of capital. The world's money markets are open 24 hours per day and it is now possible to move capital at the click of a mouse. Geography, space, and time disappear in the movement of capital in capital markets across the world.

Boundaries are of decreasing significance not only for the movement of capital but also for the movement of goods, people, services, ideas, values, and diseases. These boundaries are also of decreasing significance to the character of the environment. Emissions from states everywhere, mainly in the North, contribute to global warming and to changing weather patterns in all parts of the world. Global warming particularly threatens island states, with rising sea levels threatening the entire beach-front of the Caribbean.

Globalization also means that boundaries are of decreasing significance to the dynamics of politics. The politics of any one country cannot be fully understood without discussing the politics of another country. In short, globalization means boundaries are of decreasing significance to the dynamics of economics, politics, and culture.

Globalization could be argued to have started when trade began, because people have been moving across geographical distances and connecting with one another for many centuries. However, there are three aspects of globalization from the 1990s and beyond that make this stage of globalization fundamentally new: (1) revolutionary technologies; (2) the presence of new political influences; and (3) new policies. These create opportunities as well as adversities that we now face in the Caribbean.

REVOLUTIONARY TECHNOLOGIES

Technological advances, primarily those related to transport, have made travel cheaper and increased the possibilities for movement from one country to another (for example, jet aircraft). Technologies of communication have also been dramatically transformed by the telephone, fax machine, cellular telephone, and cable television. The telephone has reduced international distance between countries and people. In 1990, 33 billion minutes of international calls were made. In 1996, this number had increased to 70 billion. The number of international calls per person from the Caribbean was greater on average than anywhere else in the world in the mid-1990s, approximately 74 minutes per person. The average for all developing countries in the entire world was 3 minutes. For the industrial countries the average was 41 minutes per person and the global average was 11 minutes per person.

These new technologies of communication and transportation have had a profound impact on the Caribbean. First, they have facilitated the development of a new Caribbean citizen who is more exposed through travel, more informed, more aware, and less deferential. As a result, the new Caribbean citizen has greater potential for self-realization and self-development.

These new technologies also facilitated the development of the travel industry. In 1980, 261 million people in the world travelled as tourists. This was 6 percent of the world population at that time. By 2000 (20 years later) almost 700 million people travelled as tourists – almost tripling in 20 years. Approximately 10 percent of the world's population now travels as tourists. The Caribbean is as well positioned as any other part of the world to benefit from this classic industry of globalization.

Some aspects of these technologies have negative impacts:

1. They facilitate greater ease of transmission of materialist consumer values dominant in late-twentieth-century American society, where money comes to be regarded as the "be all and end all" and the possession of consumer durables as more important than other aspects of life. It could be argued that one reason why Jamaica has greater levels of materialism and of consumerism than Trinidad, for example, is because of the greater proximity of Jamaica to the US market, communication and other media.

2. The travel/tourism industry which is at the heart of globalization and which gives our region a huge advantage over other parts of the world, is extremely volatile, not only because of man-made action such as international terrorism, but as a result of weather conditions. What this means is that it is very unwise to hitch an entire economic development plan to the travel/tourism industry, even with such a big advantage. Despite its growth over the years it, nevertheless, is subject to ups and downs.

POLITICAL INFLUENCES

The second aspect of globalization that is relatively new at this stage of the process is the presence of new institutional actors on the stage of politics. This means that the state is no longer the main player. The state now has competition at the local, national level and most of all at the global or transnational level. There are 190 states, including the 13 CARICOM states. Each of these states now has to reckon with each other and with other important players in the fields of politics and economics.

1. The international governmental organizations (IGOs). These organizations include, for example, the World Bank, the International Monetary Fund and, without doubt most important of all, the World Trade Organization. The IGOs are constituted by governments coming together and forming new institutions, which then have power to one extent or another over each of the states involved. The main point is that the individual state now has to take into account a new set of IGOs, whose numbers are growing with each passing week. At the beginning of the last century, in 1909, there were about 30 IGOs; at the beginning of this century there are about 300, reflecting the growth of such organizations.
2. The international non-government organizations (NGOs). The best examples of these are the World Council of Churches, the International Confederation of Free Trade Unions and, most recently, Amnesty International, which campaigns on issues of human rights, such as capital punishment. Contemporary globalization presents increasingly powerful NGOs that the state now has to take into account. Jubilee 2000, for example, represents a network of church and religious people across different countries that campaigned for reduction and ultimately cancellation of the foreign debt owed by the most highly indebted third world states. This organization has members from over 60 different countries and cannot be ignored by the powerful industrial states – the United States, Germany, France, and Britain. In fact, some of the debt relief conceded in 2001 resulted, in part, from the campaign carried out by this transnational NGO. In 1909 there were approximately 170 international NGOs; at the end of the century, 44,000 of them existed. It can be seen that such a proliferation would not be possible without the new technologies of communication that allow people to link with one another and mobilize across states, regions, and continents.
3. The transnational corporations. These are private firms that are no longer confined to any one nation but, rather, stretch their production, marketing, lines of distribution, and acquisition of

raw materials across many different countries, hence the term multinational or transnational. On the last count, in the year 2000, there were approximately 53,000 transnational corporations, with almost 700,000 branches or affiliates across the world. These corporations are huge economic powers, so huge that very often they control more capital than the entire production of states or combinations of states. For example, General Motors, one of the largest of the American transnational corporations, in the mid-1990s generated sales revenue of US$164 billion, compared to Jamaica's GDP of approximately US $5 billion. General Motors sales revenue is more than the GDP of all the CARICOM states together, combined with the Central American countries – Costa Rica, Guatemala, and El Salvador.

In the context of globalization, therefore, the state must maintain very complex relationships with the IGOs, international NGOs, and the transnationals and its supreme authority has to be exercised in the context of other authorities such as the World Trade Organization. For example, recall the struggle that Jamaica and the entire Caribbean has had to wage with one of the transnational corporations in telecommunications (Cable and Wireless), in order to move from a situation where Cable and Wireless had a monopoly to one in which Cable and Wireless had to facilitate competition. The transnational corporations are becoming bigger because of mergers and acquisitions, for example, Chrysler and Daimler in the automobile industry. The reason for these mergers is that the bigger the blocks of capital, the more the possibility of investment in new technologies, as well as in research and development, ultimately leading to reduced cost and higher quality of goods and services. These developments have positive and negatives effects on the independent states of the Caribbean.

1. Positive effects:
   - The main positive impact of globalization is that in the economic sphere foreign direct investment is now more available to create employment, generate income, and transfer technology. However, the more efficient technology becomes, the less unskilled labour is likely to be required. For example, the manufacturers of Red Stripe Beer™, with much new investment and state-of-the-art technology, are producing more beer at a cheaper price and penetrating global markets more effectively with 300 workers, than eight years ago, when the company had 1,400 workers but were less globally competitive.
   - The second major positive is that this new dimension of globalization facilitates the building of coalitions and alliances, such as Jubilee 2000, which strengthens the ability of the disadvantaged

communities and weaker states to stand up for issues of justice, environmental protection, and human rights in a world of unequal power.

- It is creating, particularly for the Caribbean, a transnational community, out of most of its citizens who live outside its borders. This is a big advantage in terms of the ability of the Caribbean to influence state power in countries such as the United States and the United Kingdom, whose actions are very important for our survival.

2. Negatives:
   - In these organizations, power is very unevenly distributed, to the disadvantage of smaller states and poorer countries. This imbalance of power means that on critical issues most of the time these new players in globalization will take positions adverse to the interests of the smaller states, the more vulnerable economies, and the poorer countries.
   - There is lack of transparency and accountability in how these global organizations work. Many of these institutions are not accountable to those in the global population affected by their decisions. For example, the decisions of the WTO affect people in every country but the people in these countries have no mechanisms to make the WTO accountable to them.

NEW POLICIES

The third new dimension of this present stage of globalization relates to new policies. The policies of this phase of globilization are summed up by one of two words – liberalization or neo-liberalism. The policies associated with liberalization and neo-liberalism became dominant globally after the 1980s.

1. These policies required states around the world to implement two fundamental changes: the first is that states, to one degree or another, must lower and ultimately remove national barriers to the movement of capital; second, they must reduce or remove barriers to competition across states and within states with regard to the movement of goods and services. The dimension that has gone furthest fastest is financial liberalization. Capital markets are now more or less global.
2. The states were pressured to reduce the role of government in the operation of market forces, to refrain from regulating prices, and sell assets. In other words, the idea of the minimalist state took over from the idea of the welfare state. This globalization of the minimalist state was the result of pressure from the IGOs, particularly the IMF, World Bank, and WTO.

In conclusion, these two defining features of the world between 1930 and 1980 are disappearing. First, the protected market and preferential arrangements are vanishing from which developing states derived some benefit. During this period markets for sugar, banana, rice, and rum, for example, were protected, thereby giving preferential access to producers. Production developed without regard for competitiveness, because there was a guaranteed market. With the disappearance of the guaranteed market, producers who have not adjusted are are at risk in the open, competitive market.

Second, big government acting on behalf of the welfare of the people is being significantly reduced. Welfare and service increasingly are available primarily only to those who can pay for them. Educational and health services, for example, are no longer relatively free but involve "cost-sharing". The cost is shared so the government no longer has to foot all of the bills.

Positive Features of the New Policies

The reduction of barriers to trade and the growth of competition facilitates greater market access by enterprises that can be competitive. Businesses that can reduce their costs and improve their quality now have much more opportunity, not only in the domestic market but also in markets around the world.

This is one of the reasons why, in areas in which the Caribbean has already demonstrated a degree of competitiveness there is the potential of doing very well. Indeed some of the approximately 60,000 transnational corporations are Caribbean-owned (Sandals and Super Clubs, for example). Because of the nature of their services and the quality of their products they are expanding beyond individual territories into the non-English-speaking Caribbean and into South America.

Entertainment services is another area in which the Caribbean has potential for global reach. Caribbean entertainers who recognize the opportunities are taking hold of them to earn and form alliances that are not only beneficial to themselves but to others as well. For example, Shocking Vibes has entered into a very lucrative alliance with Virgin Records (one of the largest transnational corporations in the recording industry).

Information technology services is another area in which the Caribbean has some potential. Manufacturing, mainly in food and beverage (for example Red Stripe™ and various brands of rum produced around the region), has huge market potential outside the Caribbean. However, being able to fulfil that market potential depends on being cost competitive and quality reliable.

In addition, greater success for manufacturers, farmers, workers, and producers in the Caribbean and across the developing world depends in large measure on the industrialized states being pressured to make the global playing field more level. In particular, the governments of developed countries need to subsidize their own producers less and to lower tariff and non-tariff barriers to goods coming in from developing states.

Negative Features of the New Policies

Where the goods or services cannot compete, either in the domestic market or in the export market, then the prospects are closure or reducing the number of employees. For example, at J. Wray and Nephew in November 2001, about 50 workers were made redundant because the company introduced a very up-to-date technology that produces more bottled rum in less time with far fewer workers. In the United States, in the first three quarters of 2001 over 1.1 million workers were made redundant.

The most immediate implications for the Caribbean relates to traditional agricultural and other export industries, such as the sugar, banana, and rice industries, which were formed and matured based on protection. For decades cost and quality were not critical because the markets to which they sold were protected. All of this is going to end with the liberalized policies of globalization. In fact, protection for these traditional export industries in the European market will end at the latest in 2008. Unless these industries can be transformed or new industries developed to take their places, the districts and villages that depend on these traditional earnings will be in serious trouble. Preparing to become more competitive (even as we seek greater equity) is the more urgent with the likely reduction of trade barriers among the 34 states of the Western Hemisphere with the establishment of the Free Trade Area of the Americas (FTAA) planned for Janurary 1, 2005.

Because liberalization means freer trade, the danger of illicit trafficking in narcotics (particularly in cocaine) and weapons has increased. It is estimated that the value of the illicit narcotics that passed through the Caribbean prior to September 11, 2001 was US$50 billion. Therefore, we can see the potential of the proceeds of the illegal trade in drugs not only to finance international terrorist groups but also to buy political influence by providing funds for political leaders and for bribing customs, police, and military personnel. For example, in Colombia, one of the leaders of the main transnational drug operations, Pablo Escobar, was a member of a Colombian Parliament and at one time, a large percentage of the members of the Colombian Congress was in the pay of the drug cartels.

Looking at the overall picture of the impact of this present stage of the process of globalization, there can be no doubt that globalization as it is now organized has encouraged the growth of inequality, within and between countries, as those who are strong are better able to capitalize on the processes of globalization. As competition becomes more acute, all other standards and restraints become threatened. For example, one of the human rights in the United Nations Declaration of Rights is the right to freedom of association – to join and to belong to a party or trade union. Increasingly as the drive to get the cheapest possible labour to become more competitive intensifies, the drive to use child labour, non-unionized and even semi-slave labour increases around the world. The erosion of environmental standards is another danger of increasing competitiveness in a liberalized, free market environment.

On balance, the liberal policies of globalization have had a predominantly negative effect on most of the world's people and therefore, increasingly, within the last ten years and especially within the last five years, there has developed significant popular resistance to neo-liberal globalization. The basic view of people who resist globalization is not that the technologies of globalization should be reversed but, rather, that globalization should be transformed in order to protect the disadvantaged and ensure that competition does not undermine the rights of children and labour. In addition they want to ensure that environmental standards are observed. This movement also seeks to ensure that the international organizations (IGOs, international NGOs, and transnational corporations) become more accountable, more transparent, and more democratic. In this way and primarily through "pressure from below", it is hoped to transform globalization from being primarily beneficial to the few to being more advantageous to the majority of mankind.

It is in this context that we can summarize the policies that would be most appropriate to the Caribbean at the present time. First, the governments and people of the Caribbean should become more involved in forming alliances and coalitions, developing networks at the government and non-governmental levels to transform the present character of globalization; to transform current policies so they are more balanced and more equitable; and to transform the organizations of globalization to make them more balanced and more accountable.

Caribbean people resident in the United States and the United Kingdom are important constituents in very many electoral districts with voting power. We have not even begun to scratch the surface of relationships with Caribbean residents overseas in order to strengthen our bargaining power with those countries and governments.

Second, at the same time that we form new alliances there is no alternative to making our production of goods and services less costly and of a higher quality, and thereby able to keep the domestic market as well as to penetrate the overseas market. In order to accomplish this, two subsidiary requirements are important:

1. Each of the territories in our region needs to develop greater national unity, greater consensus among the presently divided segments – between labour and capital, among the political parties, and in civil society. Greater cohesion is needed at the national level in order to fulfil the requirements of competing more effectively.
2. The need for greater regional integration is recognized in almost every region of the world. At present, there are over 20 regional unions, the European Union being the most advanced. CARI-COM is one such regional body and it is absolutely essential for this regional integration to be strengthened, to create a single market across the region and ultimately create a single economy. Only in this context can we begin to find the blocks of capital (through merging small enterprises into larger units) that can begin to access the opportunities in the global marketplace in this present phase of globalization.

We are at a crucial moment in history and therefore we have no choice but to combine our efforts to make the process of globalization more balanced and equitable at the same time as we make ourselves better able to survive and to develop within an unequal world.

APPENDIX

Introduction to Political Institutions

SAMPLE OF PAST EXAMINATIONS

The following are sample examination questions set between 1999 and 2002 for students taking the course Introduction to Political Institutions (GT11A) on the Mona campus of the University of the West Indies.

The duration of each examination was two hours. Each candidate sitting the exam was required to answer two questions, each counting for 35 percent towards the final mark. The remaining 30 percent was from the course work. These questions are particularly related to the text of this book and to additional readings provided for students of the course.

April/May 2002

1. Do mass protests produce more harm than good? In developing your answer, draw on examples from modern politics in at least **one** of the following:
    [a] any Caribbean state;
    [b] the United States (of America);
    [c] any West European state;
    [d] the transition from communism to post-communism.
2. To what extent and with what safeguards, would you be in favour of restricting freedom in the interest of combating terrorism? Use appropriate illustrations.
3. How far is "people rule" being undermined by money power in American politics?
4. Blair's constitutional reforms leave the power of the British prime minister untouched. Critically discuss.
5. Caribbean people have changed while the independence constitutions have not. To what extent is this statement true and what are the implications for constitutional reform?
6. Identify and discuss ways in which the Caribbean state can better survive and develop under globalization.

December 2001

1. Do increases in "unconventional political participation" indicate a breaking down or strengthening of democracy? Use illustrations from at least one country.
2. Identify and critically discuss limits on "people rule" in American democracy.
3. Of the reforms instituted by the Blair government, say which you regard as more important and why?
4. How far has post-communism succeeded?
5. What can be done to make the Caribbean prime minister less of an "elected dictator"?
6. Is globalization good or bad for the Caribbean? Use illustrations from at least one Caribbean territory.

April/May 2001

1. To what extent and why is there a gap between Caribbean political culture and Caribbean political behaviour? Use illustrations from any one Caribbean territory.
2. In order to be a democracy, what if anything, does a country need to have besides fair and free elections? Use appropriate illustrations.
3. "Democracy for the few." "People rule." Which of these two phrases better sums up American government and politics?
4. Critically discuss Prime Minister Blair's programme for renewal of parliamentary democracy in Britain.
5. Was Russia's change to post-communism too sudden?
6. Indicate measures for constitutional reform which you would support for any Caribbean territory and the reasons for your position.
7. Critically examine ways in which Caribbean states and people may reduce vulnerability to globalization.

December 2000

1. In what ways and for what reasons is Caribbean political culture changing? Discuss with reference to at least one Caribbean state.
2. "The US Elections 2000 revealed both strengths and weaknesses in the American system." Critically discuss.
3. How far are Tony Blair's constitutional reforms in Britain revolutionary?
4. Is post-communism failing? Critically discuss in relation to any **one** post-communist state.

5. Identify and justify **four** recommendations for constitutional reform which you would propose and/or support for any single Caribbean state.
6. Does globalization present more of a threat than an opportunity for the Caribbean? Draw illustrations from at least one Caribbean state.

April 2000

1. How effective is the political socialization process in the Caribbean today? Use illustrations from at least one Caribbean state.
2. Can a state be a democracy if its elections are flawed? Draw on examples from any one country.
3. Which is the greater threat to American democracy – the danger of gridlock or the power of money? Justify your conclusion.
4. Does the constitutional reform programme of the Blair government in Britain go too far or not far enough?
5. To what extent can change to an executive presidential system solve the current weaknesses of Caribbean government? Illustrate your answer with reference to any one Caribbean state.
6. How far can globalization be blamed for contemporary Caribbean problems? Draw examples from at least one Caribbean state.

December 1999

1. Do protest and demonstrations threaten or strengthen democracy? Draw on appropriate illustrations (including from any aspect of the course **Introduction to Political Institutions**) in discussing this question.
2. To what extent and in what ways is the "rule of the people" limited in the American system of democracy?
3. "When New Labour [Britain] took power in 1997, the constitution was ripe for change" (*The Economist*, November 6 1999). Why and along what lines?
4. "It has been a rough decade" (*The Economist*, November 6 1999). Do you agree with this evaluation of the period of post-communism? What are the prospects? Illustrate your answer with reference to at least one post-communist state.
5. To what extent and why in prevailing Caribbean circumstance, should constitutional reform be a priority? Discuss with reference to any one Caribbean state.
6. Using appropriate examples, recommend ways in which any Caribbean state may make globalization less of a threat and more of an opportunity.